2nd EDITION

Ventures 1

WORKBOOK

Gretchen Bitterlin   Dennis Johnson   Donna Price   Sylvia Ramirez

K. Lynn Savage (Series Editor)

CAMBRIDGE
UNIVERSITY PRESS

CAMBRIDGE
UNIVERSITY PRESS

University Printing House, Cambridge CB2 8BS, United Kingdom

One Liberty Plaza, 20th Floor, New York, NY 10006, USA

477 Williamstown Road, Port Melbourne, VIC 3207, Australia

4843/24, 2nd Floor, Ansari Road, Daryaganj, Delhi – 110002, India

79 Anson Road, #06–04/06, Singapore 079906

Cambridge University Press is part of the University of Cambridge.

It furthers the University's mission by disseminating knowledge in the pursuit of education, learning and research at the highest international levels of excellence.

www.cambridge.org
Information on this title: www.cambridge.org/9781107628595

First published 2008
20 19 18 17 16 15 14 13 12 11 10

Printed in Mexico by Editorial Impresora Apolo, S.A. de C.V.

A catalogue record for this publication is available from the British Library

ISBN 978-1-107-69289-3 Student's Book with Audio CD
ISBN 978-1-107-62859-5 Workbook with Audio CD
ISBN 978-1-139-89720-4 Online Workbook
ISBN 978-1-107-67904-7 Teacher's Edition with Audio CD / CD-ROM
ISBN 978-1-107-61822-0 Class Audio CDs
ISBN 978-1-107-65841-7 Presentation Plus

Additional resources for this publication at www.cambridge.org/ventures

Art direction, book design, photo research, and layout services: Q2A / Bill Smith
Audio production: CityVox, LLC

Contents

Welcome

Meet your classmates

A Look at the picture. Check the names you see.

✓	Marie	___	Bao
___	Fabrice	___	Claudia
___	Abdi	___	Binh
___	Wendy	___	Carlos

B Look at the picture in A. Write the names in the correct place.

Women's Names	Men's Names
Wendy	

Check your answers. See page 132.

2 The alphabet

A Write the letters.

A _a_   B ____   ____ c   ____ d

E ____   ____ f   G ____   ____ h

____ i   J ____   K ____   ____ l

____ m   N ____   ____ o   P ____

Q ____   ____ r   ____ s   T ____

____ u   ____ v   W ____   X ____

____ y   Z ____

TRACK 2

B Listen. Write the letters.

1. R a _f_ a e l

2. ____ e t e r

3. S a c h ____

4. F ____ o r e

5. A s ____ d

6. ____ e n a

Check your answers. See page 132.

3 Numbers

A Write the letters. Then write the numbers.

<u>_o_</u> ne   <u>_1_</u>   ____ w o   ____

____ h r e e   ____   ____ o u r   ____

____ i v e   ____   ____ i x   ____

____ e v e n   ____   ____ i g h t   ____

____ i n e   ____   ____ e n   ____

B Look at the pictures. Write the words.

1. ____ _three_ ____

2. _____

3. _____

4. _____

5. _____

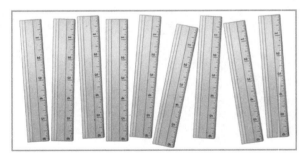

6. _____

Check your answers. See page 132.

4 Days and months

A Match.

Sunday —————— Tues.

Monday   Sat.

Tuesday   Mon.

Wednesday   Fri.

Thursday ——————Sun.

Friday   Thurs.

Saturday   Wed.

B Write the days.

January

Sunday	_____	_____	Wednesday	Thursday	_____	_____
	1	2	3	4	5	6
7	8	9	10	11	12	13

C Write the months in the correct order.

April	December	January	June	May	October
August	February	July	March	November	September

1. _____   7. _____

2. _____   8. _____

3. _____   9. _____

4. _____ *April* _____   10. _____

5. _____   11. _____

6. _____   12. _____

Check your answers. See page 132.

Personal information

LESSON A Listening

1 Write the words.

| area | first | last | middle | telephone | zip |

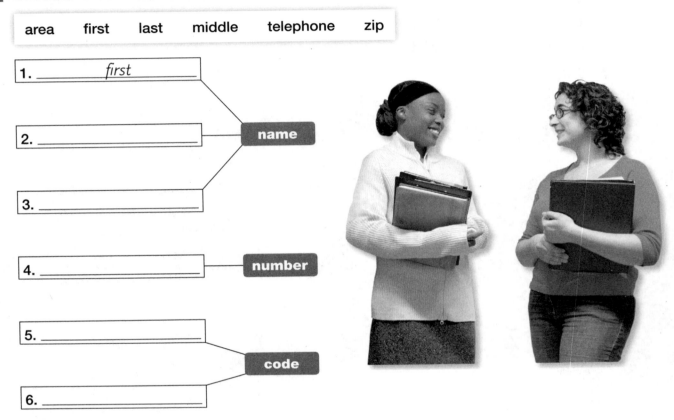

1. _____*first*_____

2. _____] name

3. _____

4. _____ — number

5. _____

6. _____] code

2 Write the words.

| area code | last name | telephone number |
| first name | middle name | zip code |

1. (Linda) May Parker _____*first name*_____
2. (718)-555-1234 _____
3. Linda May (Parker) _____
4. 718-(555-1234) _____
5. Linda (May) Parker _____
6. New York, NY (10012) _____

Check your answers. See page 132.

3 Match the questions with the answers.

1. What is your name? _b_
2. What is your first name? ____
3. What is your last name? ____
4. What is your zip code? ____
5. What is your telephone number? ____

a. 10012
b. Yuki Yamamoto
c. 555-1234
d. Yamamoto
e. Yuki

4 Look at the address book. Listen. Then write the number of the conversation.

TRACK 3

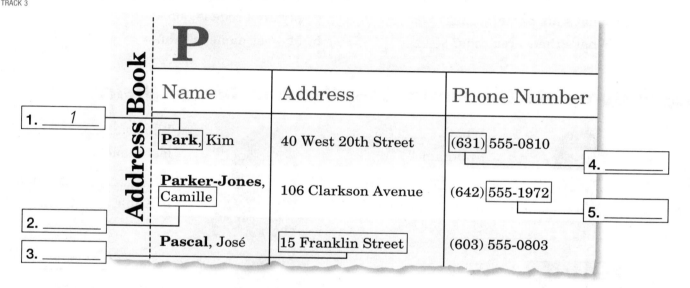

5 Write the numbers.

1. (six three one) five five five – seven eight one zero

   _(631) 555-7810_

2. (six four two) five five five – one nine seven two

   _____

3. (four three two) five five five – nine eight zero three

   _____

4. (seven nine eight) five five five – six four two one

   _____

Check your answers. See page 132.

LESSON B What's your name?

Study the chart on page 127.

1 Match the questions with the answers.

1. What's his middle name? _f_
2. What's her telephone number? ____
3. What's your last name? ____
4. What's their zip code? ____
5. What's her first name? ____
6. What's your area code? ____
7. What's his name? ____
8. What's their area code? ____

a. Their zip code is 85713.
b. Her first name is Jenna.
c. Her telephone number is 555-2758.
d. His name is Asad.
e. Their area code is 512.
f. His middle name is James.
g. My area code is 305.
h. My last name is Tran.

2 Complete the sentences. Use *her*, *his*, or *their*.

1. **A** What's _____his_____ first name?

   B _____His_____ first name is Hong-zhi.

2. **A** What's _____ area code?

   B _____ area code is 808.

3. **A** What's _____ last name?

   B _____ last name is Kulik.

4. **A** What's _____ telephone number?

   B _____ telephone number is 555-1850.

3 Read the advertisement. Circle the answers.

1. What is Tina's last name?
   a. Jane
   b.) Rodriguez

2. What is Tina's area code?
   a. 555
   b. 415

3. What is Tina's telephone number?
   a. (415) 555-8221
   b. (415) 555-9221

> ### Job Wanted
>
> **Babysitter for Hire**
> Tina Jane Rodriguez: Experienced
> mother and child-care worker.
> San Francisco area.
> Call Tina at
> (415) 555-8221.

Check your answers. See page 132.

4 **Complete the sentences. Use _her_, _his_, or _their_. Then listen.**

TRACK 4

1. _A_ What's _____*his*_____ name?

   _B_ _____ name is Coach Jones.

2. _A_ What's _____ name?

   _B_ _____ name is Mrs. Jones.

3. _A_ What's _____ name?

   _B_ _____ name is the Eagles.

5 **Look at the pictures. Write sentences.**

1. John Brown-Hudson
   His name is John
   Brown-Hudson.
   (name)

2. Mary Wilson
   _____
   _____
   (first name)

3. Mr. and Mrs. Lopez
   _____
   _____
   (last name)

4. (608) 555-1234
   _____
   (area code)

5. 02455
   _____
   (zip code)

6. 555-1234
   _____
   (telephone number)

LESSON **C** Are you from Canada?

Study the chart on page 126.

1 **Complete the sentences. Use contractions.**

1. ___We're___ from Canada.
(We are)

2. _____ from Japan.
(They are)

3. _____ from Russia.
(He is)

4. _____ from Somalia.
(She is)

5. _____ from Korea.
(I am)

6. _____ from Brazil.
(They are)

2 **Write sentences.**

1. from / She's / Ecuador / . _She's from Ecuador._____

2. China / He's / from / . _____

3. He / from / Korea / isn't / . _____

4. They're / Colombia / from / . _____

5. India / You're / from / . _____

6. Mexico / from / They're / . _____

7. They / Russia / from / aren't / . _____

8. She / isn't / Brazil / from / . _____

9. You / from / aren't / Japan / . _____

10. the United States / She's / from / . _____

Check your answers. See page 132.

3 Look at the pictures. Answer the questions.

China

1. **A** Is he from Brazil?

   B ___No___, ___he___ ___isn't___ .

2. **A** Is he from China?

   B _____, _____ _____ .

Korea

3. **A** Is she from the United States?

   B _____, _____ _____ .

4. **A** Is she from Korea?

   B _____, _____ _____ .

Mexico

5. **A** Are you from Peru?

   B _____, _____ _____ .

6. **A** Are you from Mexico?

   B _____, _____ _____ .

India

7. **A** Are they from Somalia?

   B _____, _____ _____ .

8. **A** Are they from India?

   B _____, _____ _____ .

4 Complete the sentences. Use *am*, *are*, or *is*. Then listen.

TRACK 5

1. **A** What ___is___ your last name?

   B My last name _____ Sanchez.

2. **A** _____ you from the United States?

   B No, I _____ from Mexico.

3. **A** _____ she from the United States?

   B Yes, she _____ .

4. **A** Where _____ Mariya and Ivan from?

   B They _____ from Russia.

5. **A** What _____ their last name?

   B Their last name _____ Chernov.

6. **A** What _____ her telephone number?

   B Her telephone number _____ 555-9763.

Check your answers. See page 132.

LESSON D Reading

1 Find the words.

address	city	signature	street	zip code
apartment	initial	state	title	

t	i	t	l	e	m	r	a	t	i
e	n	c	i	t	y	g	a	i	a
z	i	p	c	o	d	e	p	i	s
s	t	t	r	u	t	n	a	s	a
s	i	g	n	a	t	u	r	e	e
n	a	i	e	s	t	a	t	e	e
n	l	e	i	n	t	n	m	d	e
d	g	e	(a	d	d	r	e	s	s)
r	r	o	a	t	a	t	n	n	y
n	n	s	t	r	e	e	t	t	a

2 Write the words from Exercise 1 on the letter.

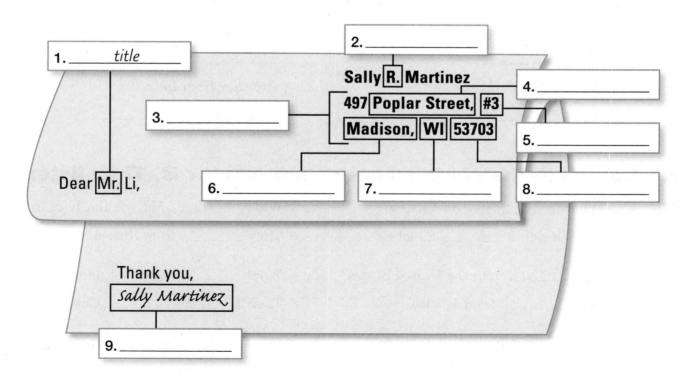

1. _____title_____

2. _____

Sally R. Martinez

4. _____

3. _____

497 Poplar Street, #3

Madison, WI 53703

5. _____

Dear Mr. Li,

6. _____

7. _____

8. _____

Thank you,

Sally Martinez

9. _____

Check your answers. See page 132.

3 Read and complete the ID card. Then listen.

TRACK 6

Juan Cabrera is a new student. He's from Colombia. His middle name is Carlos. His address is 138 Clark Avenue, Apt. 6, Tampa, Florida. His zip code is 33629. His telephone number is 555-3461. His area code is 813.

STUDENT ID

Name _____Cabrera_____ _____ _____
           Last   First   Middle

Address _____

        _____ _____ _____
           City   State   Zip code

Phone (_____) _____ - _____

4 Read the questions. Circle the correct answers.

1. What's his name?
   a. His name is Juan.
   b. My name is Juan.

2. What country is he from?
   a. He's from Colombia.
   b. I'm from Colombia.

3. What's his last name?
   a. His last name is Cabrera.
   b. Her last name is Carlos.

4. What's his area code?
   a. His area code is 555-3461.
   b. His area code is 813.

5. What's his zip code?
   a. His zip code is 813.
   b. His zip code is 33629.

6. What's his city?
   a. His city is Clark Avenue.
   b. His city is Tampa.

Check your answers. See page 132.

LESSON E Writing

1 Write sentences.

1. China / are / They / from / .
   They are from China.

2. from / Where / you / are / ?
   _____

3. is / her / middle name / Mary / .
   _____

4. is / My / zip code / 92122 / .
   _____

5. you / spell / How / do / that / ?
   _____

6. His / 1241 Washington Avenue / is / address / .
   _____

7. is / telephone number / What / your / ?
   _____

8. 202 / Their / is / area code / .
   _____

2 Correct the sentences. Add capital letters.

1.   H   B J
   his name is bill jackson.

2. he is a new student.

3. his address is 371 purdy avenue.

4. his telephone number is 555-7819.

5. he is from new york.

Check your answers. See pages 132–133.

3 Read the business card. Complete the sentences.

Premier Landscaping
Large or small, we do it all.

John C. Gonzalez
57 Bridge Road
Orange Park, FL 32073
(559) 555-7579

| address | area code | last name | middle initial | telephone number | zip code |

1. His ___*last name*___ is Gonzalez.
2. His _____ is 559.
3. His _____ is 32073.
4. His _____ is 555-7579.
5. His _____ is 57 Bridge Road.
6. His _____ is C.

4 Write a conversation. Use the sentences in the box.

Speaker A	Speaker B
My telephone number is (545) 555-7771.	Hi, Terri. What's your last name?
I'm Terri.	Thanks. We'll call you soon.
My last name is Smith.	OK. What's your telephone number?

1. *A* __*I'm Terri.*_____

2. *B* _____

3. *A* _____

4. *B* _____

5. *A* _____

6. *B* _____

Check your answers. See page 133.

LESSON F Another view

1 Look at the student ID. Answer the questions.

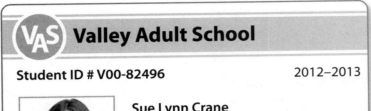

Valley Adult School

Student ID # V00-82496   2012–2013

Sue Lynn Crane
350 Hudson Avenue, #4A
Pasadena, CA 91109
DOB: 4-17-1990

Sue L. Crane

Abbreviations
ID = identification
# = number
DOB = date of birth

1. What's her first name? _Sue_____

2. What's her school? _____

3. What's her zip code? _____

4. What's her student ID number? _____

5. What's her street? _____

6. What's her middle initial? _____

7. What's her city? _____

8. What's her last name? _____

9. What's her apartment number? _____

2 Look at the information in Exercise 1. Fill in the correct answers.

1. What's your first name?
   ● My first name is Sue.
   Ⓑ My first name is Lynn.
   Ⓒ My first name is Crane.
   Ⓓ My first name is Hudson.

2. What's your last name?
   Ⓐ My last name is Sue.
   Ⓑ My first name is Lynn.
   Ⓒ My last name is Crane.
   Ⓓ My last name is Hudson.

3. What's your zip code?
   Ⓐ My zip code is 82496.
   Ⓑ My zip code is 91109.
   Ⓒ My zip code is 91190.
   Ⓓ My zip code is 1990.

4. What's your address?
   Ⓐ Pasadena, CA, #4A
   Ⓑ 91109 Valley Avenue, #4A
   Ⓒ 350 Hudson Avenue, #4A
   Ⓓ 350 Hudson Avenue, #4-17-1990

Check your answers. See page 133.

3 **Complete the sentences. Then match the sentences to the picture.**

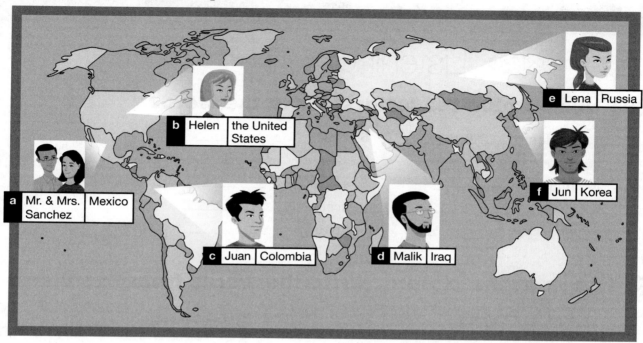

1. _____*Her*_____ name is Helen. _____*She's*_____ from the United States. __*b*__

2. _____ name is Juan. _____ from Colombia. ____

3. _____ name is Jun. _____ from Korea. ____

4. _____ name is Malik. _____ from Iraq. ____

5. _____ name is Sanchez. _____ from Mexico. ____

6. _____ name is Lena. _____ from Russia. ____

4 **Answer the questions.**

A What's your name?

B _____

A Where are you from?

B _____

Check your answers. See page 133.

LESSON **A** Listening

1 **Unscramble the letters. Write the words.**

1. laccrlauto _calculator_
2. oobk _____
3. clipne _____
4. pma _____
5. bleat _____

6. kcclo _____
7. dkse _____
8. sreear _____
9. koobteno _____
10. lurre _____

2 **Look at the picture. Write the words from Exercise 1.**

1. _____
2. _____
3. _____
4. _____
5. _____
6. _____
7. _____
8. _____
9. _____
10. _____

Check your answers. See page 133.

3 Look at the picture in Exercise 2. Write.

| book | calculator | eraser | notebook | pencil | ruler |

On the table
calculator
_____

Under the desk
_____
_____

In the desk
_____
_____

4 Listen. Circle the correct letters.

TRACK 7

1. (a.)    b.

2. a.  b.

3. a.  b.

4. a.  b.

5. a.   b.

Check your answers. See page 133.

LESSON B Where is the pen?

1 **Look at the pictures. Write the words. Then circle *in*, *on*, or *under*.**

calculator	calendar	computer	dictionary	eraser	ruler

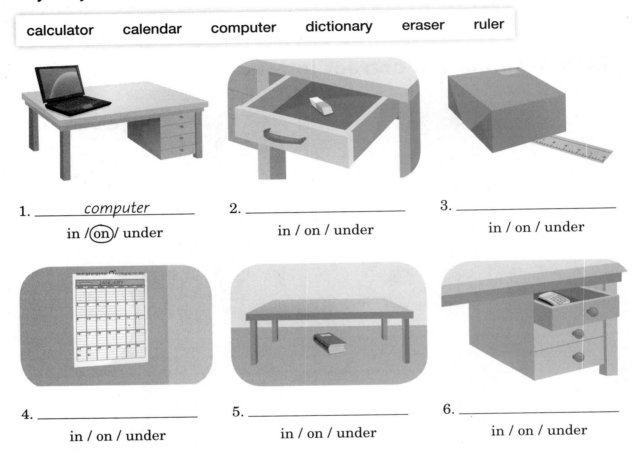

1. _____*computer*_____
in /(on)/ under

2. _____
in / on / under

3. _____
in / on / under

4. _____
in / on / under

5. _____
in / on / under

6. _____
in / on / under

2 **Look at the picture. Circle the correct answers.**

1. Excuse me. Where's the computer?
   (a.) It's on the desk.
   b. It's under the desk.

2. Where's the clock?
   a. It's on the desk.
   b. It's on the wall.

3. Where's the pencil?
   a. It's under the dictionary.
   b. It's in the drawer.

4. Where's the ruler?
   a. It's under the dictionary.
   b. It's on the dictionary.

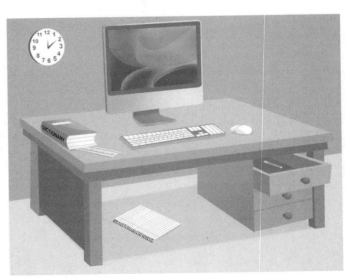

Check your answers. See page 133.

3 Look at the picture. Complete the sentences with *in*, *on*, or *under*.

1. **A** Where's the calculator?

    B It's ____on____ the table.

2. **A** Where's the calendar?

    B It's _____ the wall.

3. **A** Where's the book?

    B It's _____ the cabinet.

4. **A** Where's the notebook?

    B It's _____ the table.

4 Look at the picture in Exercise 3. Write questions and answers. Use *in*, *on*, or *under*.

1. **A** *Where's the pencil?*
       (pencil)

    B *It's on the table.*
       (table)

2. **A** _____
       (eraser)

    B _____
       (table)

3. **A** _____
       (ruler)

    B _____
       (box)

4. **A** _____
       (clock)

    B _____
       (cabinet)

5 Listen and number the sentences in the correct order.

TRACK 8

_____ In the cabinet?

_____ Thank you.

__1__ Excuse me. Where's the dictionary?

_____ You're welcome.

_____ Yes. It's in the cabinet.

_____ It's in the cabinet.

Check your answers. See page 133.

1 Look at the pictures. Write the words.

cabinet   desks   dictionary   erasers   notebooks   pencils   rulers

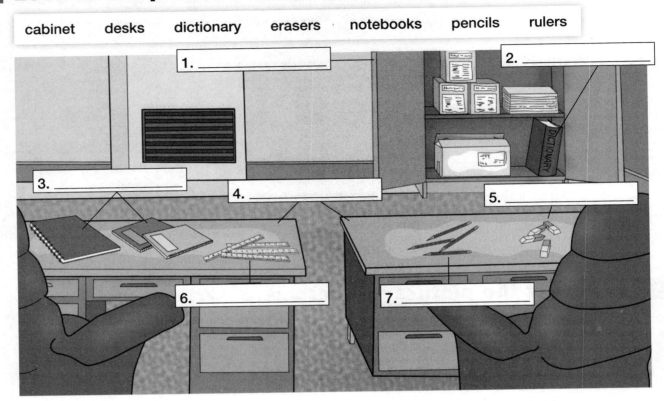

1. _____

2. _____

3. _____

4. _____

5. _____

6. _____

7. _____

books   calculator   calendar   clocks   computers   map   table

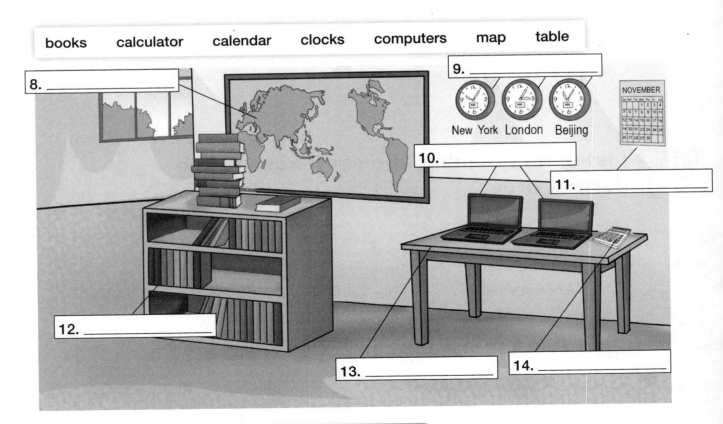

8. _____

9. _____

10. _____

11. _____

12. _____

13. _____

14. _____

Check your answers. See page 133.

2 Complete the charts. Use the words from Exercise 1.

Singular nouns	
cabinet	

Plural nouns	
desks	

3 Complete the sentences. Use *it is*, *it isn't*, *they are*, or *they aren't*.

1. **A** Are the calendars on the table?

   B Yes, _____they are_____.

2. **A** Is the ruler in the box?

   B No, _____.

3. **A** Are the computers in the classroom?

   B Yes, _____.

4. **A** Is the eraser under the desk?

   B Yes, _____.

5. **A** Are the maps on the wall?

   B No, _____.

6. **A** Is the pencil in the drawer?

   B No, _____.

7. **A** Are the books in the cabinet?

   B Yes, _____.

8. **A** Are the pens on the filing cabinet?

   B Yes, _____.

9. **A** Is the notebook under the desk?

   B No, _____.

10. **A** Are the calculators on the table?

    B Yes, _____.

4 Write sentences.

1. **A** Where / the calculators / are / ?

   Where are the calculators?

   B are / They / on / the desk / .

   _____

2. **A** the book / under / Is / the table / ?

   _____

   B isn't / No, / it / .

   _____

Check your answers. See page 133.

UNIT 2   23

LESSON D Reading

1 Find the words.

dictionary	laptop	notebook	rulers	stapler
eraser	marker	notepads	scissors	whiteboard

```
o  s  w  x  i  b  n  s  u  r  h  l
y  t  r  j  t  t  z  j  u  h  s  n
w  a  l  c  m  a  r  k  e  r  c  j
h  p  w  r  u  l  e  r  s  b  i  w
i  l  s  g  g  u  x  x  v  n  s  x
t  e  n  o  t  e  p  a  d  s  s  f
e  r  e  m  z  s  d  y  x  x  o  i
b  u  d  i  c  t  i  o  n  a  r  y
o  n  o  t  e  b  o  o  k  k  s  n
a  x  y  q  z  h  v  z  w  j  t  x
r  m  d  i  v  e  r  a  s  e  r  r
d  e  l  a  p  t  o  p  y  h  k  l
```

2 Match the questions with the answers.

1. Are the index cards on the top shelf? _f_

2. Is the marker in the box? ____

3. Is the ruler on the table? ____

4. Are the calculators in the cabinet? ____

5. Is the notebook in the drawer? ____

6. Is the stapler on the desk? ____

a. No, they aren't. The calculators are on the table.

b. No, it isn't. The marker is in the cabinet.

c. No, it isn't. The stapler is in the cabinet.

d. Yes, it's in the drawer.

e. Yes, it's on the table.

f. No, they aren't. The index cards are on the bottom shelf.

Check your answers. See page 133.

3 **Write a conversation. Use the sentences in the box.**

Speaker A	Speaker B
The notebooks are on the top shelf.	Thanks. I also need a pencil.
May I help you?	Good. Now I'm ready to write!
The pencils are on the bottom shelf.	Yes, please. Where are the notebooks?

1. *A* <u>May I help you?</u>

2. *B* _____

3. *A* _____

4. *B* _____

5. *A* _____

6. *B* _____

4 **Read and answer the questions. Then listen.**

TRACK 9

—————————(acme)—————————

July 6, 2012

Dear Ang,

Welcome to Acme Offices! The notepads are in the desk drawer. The pencils are in a box on the shelf. The erasers are in the box, too. The calculators are in the cabinet. The notebooks are under the calculators. The stapler is on the desk.

Sincerely,
Ms. Grant
Manager

1. Where are the notepads?   <u>The notepads are in the desk drawer.</u>

2. Where's the stapler?   _____

3. Where are the calculators?   _____

4. Where are the pencils?   _____

5. Where are the notebooks?   _____

6. Where are the erasers?   _____

Check your answers. See page 133.   **UNIT 2   25**

LESSON E Writing

1 Write sentences.

1. Where / the / books / are / ?

   Where are the books?

2. The clock / is / the wall / on / .

   _____

3. the books / Are / the cabinet / in / ?

   _____

4. are / The pencils / the desk / on / .

   _____

5. the ruler / the notebook / Is / under / ?

   _____

6. is / the laptop / Where / ?

   _____

7. The notebook / the desk / on / is / .

   _____

8. in / the drawer / Is / the stapler / ?

   _____

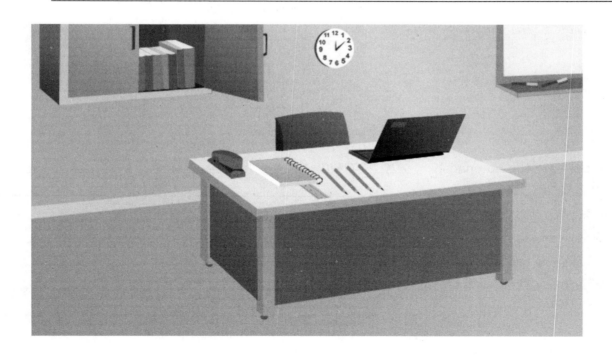

Check your answers. See page 133.

2 Circle the correct words.

1. **A** Is the map on the wall?

   B Yes, (it is) / they are.

2. **A** Are the pens in the box?

   B No, it isn't / they aren't.

3. **A** Is the notebook on the table?

   B Yes, it is / they are.

4. **A** Is the ruler on the desk?

   B No, it isn't / they aren't.

5. **A** Is the laptop on the table?

   B Yes, it is / they are.

6. **A** Are the desks in the classroom?

   B Yes, it is / they are.

7. **A** Is the whiteboard on the wall?

   B Yes, it is / they are.

8. **A** Is the dictionary under the desk?

   B No, it isn't / they aren't.

3 Add capital letters and periods. Then rewrite the corrected sentences.

1. the classroom is ready for the students

2. the books are in the cabinet

3. the map is on the wall

4. the clock is on the filing cabinet

5. the pencils are on the table

6. the laptop is on the table

7. the markers are in the drawer

8. the calculators are under the desks

1. _The classroom is ready for the students._

2. _____

3. _____

4. _____

5. _____

6. _____

7. _____

8. _____

LESSON F Another view

1 Read the questions. Look at the chart. Then fill in the correct answers.

ITEM	QUANTITY	LOCATION
notebooks	15	under the table
laptops	1	on the desk
calculators	3	on the table
rulers	2	in the drawer
pens	30	in the cabinet
pencils	30	in the cabinet
books	30	under the table

1. Where are the notebooks?
   - ● under the table
   - Ⓑ in the drawer
   - Ⓒ in the cabinet
   - Ⓓ on the desk

2. What's on the desk?
   - Ⓐ a notebook
   - Ⓑ a laptop
   - Ⓒ a ruler
   - Ⓓ a pencil

3. What are in the cabinet?
   - Ⓐ laptops and rulers
   - Ⓑ pens and books
   - Ⓒ notebooks and pencils
   - Ⓓ pens and pencils

4. How many laptops are on the desk?
   - Ⓐ 1
   - Ⓑ 2
   - Ⓒ 3
   - Ⓓ 15

5. What are under the table?
   - Ⓐ notebooks and laptops
   - Ⓑ rulers and books
   - Ⓒ notebooks and rulers
   - Ⓓ notebooks and books

6. What are on the table?
   - Ⓐ books
   - Ⓑ laptops
   - Ⓒ notebooks
   - Ⓓ calculators

7. Where are the rulers?
   - Ⓐ in the cabinet
   - Ⓑ in the drawer
   - Ⓒ on the desk
   - Ⓓ under the table

8. How many notebooks are under the table?
   - Ⓐ 1
   - Ⓑ 3
   - Ⓒ 15
   - Ⓓ 30

Check your answers. See page 134.

2 Look at the pictures. Complete the sentences.

1. _____*This is*_____ a hole puncher.
This is / That is

2. _____ erasers.
That is / Those are

3. _____ markers.
This is / These are

4. _____ a calculator.
That is / This is

5. _____ a notepad.
This is / That is

6. _____ index cards.
That is / Those are

7. _____ rulers.
These are / Those are

8. _____ a stapler.
That is / Those are

9. _____ a laptop.
This is / These are

10. _____ paper clips.
Those are / These are

Check your answers. See page 134.

Friends and family

LESSON A Listening

1 **Complete the words.**

1. <u>b</u> r o t h <u>e</u> r
2. m ____ t h e ____
3. f a ____ h ____ r
4. g ____ a ____ d f a ____ h e r
5. ____ r a n ____ m o ____ h e r
6. ____ i s ____ e r

2 **Look at the picture. Write the words from Exercise 1 in the correct places.**

Esteban

Consuela

Sylvia

Luis

Andrea

Jorge

1. ____grandfather____

2. ____

3. ____

4. ____

5. ____

6. ____

Check your answers. See page 134.

3 Complete the sentences.

daughter   grandfather   mother   son   wife

Family Photo

This is a picture of my family. Sheila is my

_____wife_____ . Next to her are James, our
1.

_____ , and Megan, our _____ .
2.   3.

Behind Sheila are her _____ and father.
4.

Megan and James love their _____
5.

and grandmother very much!

4 Listen to the conversations. Match the pictures to the people.

TRACK 10

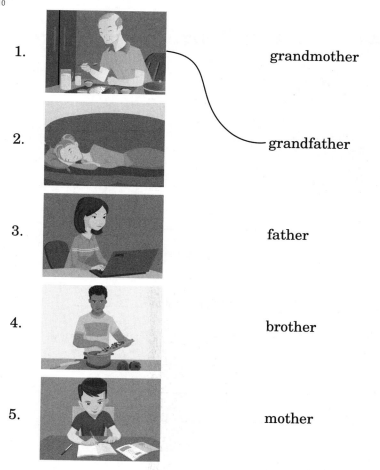

1.   grandmother

2.   grandfather

3.   father

4.   brother

5.   mother

Check your answers. See page 134.

LESSON B What are you doing?

Study the chart on page 127.

1 Complete the sentences.

1. **A** What's Mimi doing?

   B She _'s reading_____ a book.

       (read)

2. **A** What's Hsu-jing doing?

   B She _____ on the phone.

       (talk)

3. **A** What's Anatoly doing?

   B He _____ dinner.

     (cook)

4. **A** What are Irene and Jack doing?

   B They _____ popcorn.

     (eat)

5. **A** What's Pierre doing?

   B He _____ TV.

     (watch)

6. **A** What's Brenda doing?

   B She _____ to music.

     (listen)

7. **A** What are Louis and Marco doing?

   B They _____ English.

     (study)

8. **A** What's Ibrahim doing?

   B He _____.

     (sleep)

2 Read the chart. Answer the questions.

Jason's Schedule
9 a.m. study English
10 a.m. read a book
12 noon eat lunch
2 p.m. listen to music
9 p.m. watch TV

1. It's 9:00 a.m. What is Jason doing?   _He's studying English._____

2. It's 10:00 a.m. What is Jason doing?   _____

3. It's 12:00 noon. What is Jason doing?   _____

4. It's 2:00 p.m. What is Jason doing?   _____

5. It's 9:00 p.m. What is Jason doing?   _____

Check your answers. See page 134.

3 Read the e-mail. Circle the present continuous verbs.

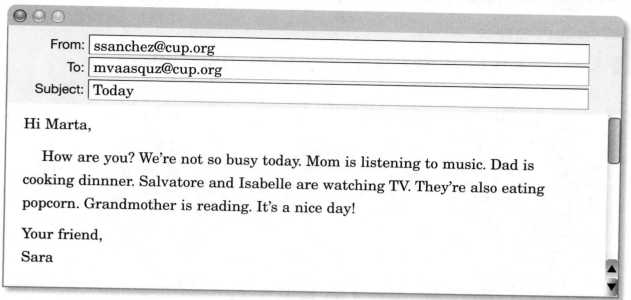

From: ssanchez@cup.org
To: mvaasquz@cup.org
Subject: Today

Hi Marta,

How are you? We're not so busy today. Mom is listening to music. Dad is cooking dinnner. Salvatore and Isabelle are watching TV. They're also eating popcorn. Grandmother is reading. It's a nice day!

Your friend,
Sara

4 Write a conversation. Use the sentences in the box. Then listen.

TRACK 11

Speaker A	Speaker B
I'm busy. I'm studying English.	What are you doing?
Hello?	Hi, Maria. This is Raul.
Oh, hi, Raul.	Oh, sorry. I'll call back later.

1. **A** _Hello?_ _____

2. **B** _____

3. **A** _____

4. **B** _____

5. **A** _____

6. **B** _____

LESSON C Are you working now?

Study the chart on page 127.

1 Look at the picture. Answer the questions.

1. Is David reading a newspaper?   _Yes, he is._

2. Is Rachel driving to work?   _____

3. Is Todd studying?   _____

4. Is Tim watching TV?   _____

5. Is Brooke listening to music?   _____

6. Are Brooke and Tim helping Rachel?   _____

7. Is Rachel taking a break?   _____

8. Is Tim talking on the telephone?   _____

2 Look at the picture in Exercise 1. Answer the questions.

1. What is Rachel doing?   _She is working._

2. What is Brooke doing?   _____

3. What is Tim doing?   _____

4. What are Todd and David doing?   _____

Check your answers. See page 134.

3 Change the answers in Exercise 2 into questions.

1. _Is she working?_

2. _____

3. _____

4. _____

4 Look and write. Then listen.

TRACK 12

1. Andrea _____*is working*_____ now.
   <u>work</u>

2. Steve _____ to work.
   <u>drive</u>

3. Consuela _____ a break.
   <u>take</u>

4. Jorge _____ Luis.
   <u>help</u>

5. Amy and Nick _____ popcorn.
   <u>eat</u>

Check your answers. See page 134.

LESSON D Reading

TRACK 13

1 Read and write the names on the family tree. Then listen.

> Javid is married to Sara. They have two children, one son and one daughter. The son's name is Omid, and the daughter's name is Avid. Omid is married to Leila. They have two sons, Daniel and Ali. Avid isn't married. She doesn't have any children.

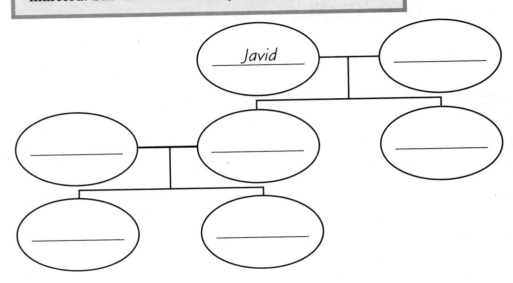

Javid

2 Read the questions. Complete the answers.

brother	grandfather	grandson	mother	son
daughter	grandmother	husband	sister	wife

1. Who is Javid? He is Sara's _____husband_____.

2. Who is Sara? She is Avid's _____.

3. Who is Leila? She is Omid's _____.

4. Who is Avid? She is Omid's _____.

5. Who is Omid? He is Avid's _____.

6. Who is Ali? He is Javid's _____.

7. Who is Avid? She is Javid's _____.

8. Who is Omid? He is Sara's _____.

9. Who is Javid? He is Daniel's _____.

10. Who is Sara? She is Ali's _____.

Check your answers. See page 134.

3 Complete the sentences.

cousin	grandmother	niece	sister-in-law
grandfather	nephew	sister	uncle

1. My mother's mother is my _____*grandmother*_____.

2. My mother's father is my _____.

3. My brother's wife is my _____.

4. My mother's brother is my _____.

5. My father's daughter is my _____.

6. My brother's daughter is my _____.

7. My sister's son is my _____.

8. My aunt's daughter is my _____.

4 Find the words.

aunt	grandfather	husband	nephew	uncle
father	grandmother	mother	niece	wife

a	o	v	h	k	k	n	h	z	o	m	r	l	r	x
m	f	b	g	g	l	v	u	z	h	k	d	g	x	n
z	f	a	d	k	m	z	s	y	s	w	i	f	e	i
o	w	j	p	o	a	s	b	i	x	b	c	j	b	e
f	a	t	h	e	r	n	a	l	z	g	a	o	v	c
q	h	h	t	h	x	w	n	g	e	r	n	n	d	e
u	e	n	m	w	e	e	d	h	o	a	e	u	d	l
r	t	w	o	d	k	l	t	h	x	n	p	a	z	o
a	u	n	t	z	i	a	s	m	u	d	h	v	e	o
n	y	s	h	q	f	g	y	n	n	f	e	c	y	f
i	t	f	e	d	s	o	d	f	u	a	w	i	o	z
x	c	r	r	q	i	c	e	a	m	t	s	m	k	s
j	o	a	y	s	u	s	w	d	a	h	z	d	e	w
u	r	w	z	q	b	u	n	c	l	e	v	v	s	e
g	r	a	n	d	m	o	t	h	e	r	n	l	c	n

Check your answers. See page 134.

LESSON **E** Writing

1 Write sentences.

1. **A** doing / . What / you / are / ?

    What are you doing? _____

    B dinner / cooking / I'm / .

    _____

2. **A** brothers / How many / do / have / you / ?

    _____

    B two / I / brothers / have / .

    _____

3. **A** you / Do / any sisters / have / ?

    _____

    B have / I / sisters / five / Yes, / .

    _____

2 Correct the sentences. Add capital letters.

1. ~~t~~oday is ana's birthday.

2. she is 15 years old.

3. ana's mother, luisa, is making a birthday cake.

4. her grandparents are wrapping presents.

5. ana is having a big party.

6. her friends are dancing at the party.

7. ana's father, reynaldo, is taking pictures.

8. they are very happy today.

Check your answers. See page 134.

3 Complete the sentences.

1. **A** What are you doing?

   B _____We're having_____ a party. It's Paul's birthday.

   (we / have)

2. **A** Who's there?

   B Well, Sally and Jim are here. _____.

   (they / talk)

3. **A** Who else is there?

   B Frank and Jane are here. _____ now.

   (they / sing)

4. **A** Is Mother there?

   B Yes, Mother is here. _____ dinner now.

   (she / cook)

5. **A** What is Paul doing?

   B _____ pictures.

   (he / take)

4 Complete the paragraph.

brother	daughter	nephew	sister
cousin	married	single	son

My name is Raul. I'm _____married_____.
                            1
My wife's name is Jane. Today is a big day. It's

Paula's birthday. She's our _____.
                                    2
She's six years old. We're having a party. Jane's

_____ Lisa is here. Lisa isn't married. She's
       3

_____, and she doesn't have any children.
       4

Lisa is putting candles on Paula's birthday cake.

My _____ Juan is here, too. He is taking
          5

pictures. Ron is here, too. He is Juan's _____.
                                                  6

Ron, my _____, is playing with Paula. Paula
               7

and her _____ are very happy today!
               8

LESSON F Another view

1 Look at the tax form. Fill in the correct answers.

Form 1			Tax Form 2013
First Name		Last Name	
Duc		**Nguyen**	
Exemptions	a. Yourself ☒		
	b. Spouse ☒		

Abbreviations
No. = Number

Dependents

First Name	Last Name	Social Security Number	Relationship
Lam	Nguyen	555-93-2458	daughter
Thanh	Nguyen	555-84-3498	son
Toan	Nguyen	555-52-1256	daughter
Lien	Le	555-32-3421	mother

Number of children who live with you **3**

Total number of exemptions claimed **6**

1020 EZ

1. How many daughters does Duc have?
   - Ⓐ 1
   - ● 2
   - Ⓒ 3
   - Ⓓ 4

2. How many children live with Duc?
   - Ⓐ 1
   - Ⓑ 2
   - Ⓒ 3
   - Ⓓ 4

3. How many sons does Duc have?
   - Ⓐ 1
   - Ⓑ 2
   - Ⓒ 3
   - Ⓓ 4

4. Who is Lien?
   - Ⓐ Duc's daughter
   - Ⓑ Duc's mother
   - Ⓒ Duc's wife
   - Ⓓ Duc's son

5. Who is Thanh?
   - Ⓐ Duc's daughter
   - Ⓑ Duc's mother
   - Ⓒ Duc's wife
   - Ⓓ Duc's son

6. Who is Lam?
   - Ⓐ Duc's daughter
   - Ⓑ Duc's mother
   - Ⓒ Duc's wife
   - Ⓓ Duc's son

Check your answers. See page 134.

2 Look at the bold word. Cross out the word that is different.

1. **mother**   ~~son~~   sister   grandmother
2. **cooking**   cleaning   daughter   studying
3. **niece**   nephew   birthday   aunt
4. **brother**   grandfather   uncle   watching
5. **reading**   listening   playing   music
6. **book**   dictionary   newspaper   TV
7. **drinking**   eating   guitar   watching
8. **husband**   wife   daughter   friend

3 Complete the sentences.

1. Sandy likes pizza, but I don't like _____*it*_____.

2. Dani knows my uncle, but Mark doesn't know _____.

3. Jason helps my sister with her homework, but I don't help _____.

4. Tony has three cats, but Sara doesn't like _____.

5. Rob eats popcorn, but Amy doesn't like _____.

6. Luis likes these books, but Marta doesn't like _____.

7. My niece likes hip-hop music, but I don't like _____.

8. Lisa knows my nephew, but Jason doesn't know _____.

LESSON A Listening

1 Find the words.

ache	back	cough	fever	sore
ankle	cold	ear	head	stomach

a	n	k	l	e	a	e	a	r
s	o	r	e	t	k	c	c	m
t	s	r	a	h	t	o	h	s
f	e	v	e	r	b	u	e	n
o	a	e	d	o	a	g	h	h
s	t	o	m	a	c	h	t	e
a	t	h	k	t	k	r	a	a
a	t	q	a	s	w	e	d	d
s	c	o	l	d	s	c	f	o

2 Complete the charts. Use the words from Exercise 1.

Parts of the body	Problems
ankle	ache

3 Match the words.

1. sore __c__
2. head ____
3. sprained ____
4. broken ____

a. ankle
b. leg
c. throat
d. ache

Check your answers. See page 135.

4 Look at the pictures. Write the words.

backache	fever	sore throat
cough	headache	stomachache

1. _____headache_____

2. _____

3. _____

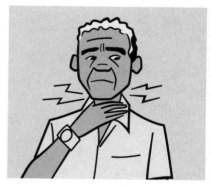

4. _____

5. _____

6. _____

5 Listen to the conversations. Then write the problem you hear.

TRACK 14

1. I have _____a headache_____.
   (a stomachache / a headache)

2. I have _____.
   (a cough / a cold)

3. I have _____.
   (a broken leg / an earache)

4. I have _____.
   (a sprained ankle / a sore throat)

5. I have _____.
   (an earache / a headache)

Check your answers. See page 135.

LESSON **B** I have a headache.

Study the chart on page 129.

1 Look at the picture. Circle the correct answers.

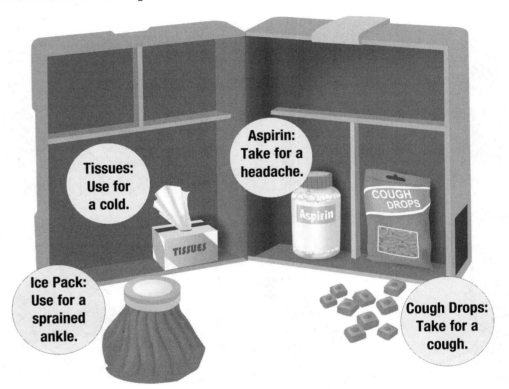

1. What do you take for a cough?
   a. aspirin
   b. an ice pack
   c. cough drops
   d. tissues

2. What do you take for a headache?
   a. aspirin
   b. an ice pack
   c. cough drops
   d. tissues

3. What do you use for a sprained ankle?
   a. aspirin
   b. an ice pack
   c. cough drops
   d. tissues

4. What do you use for a cold?
   a. aspirin
   b. an ice pack
   c. cough drops
   d. tissues

2 Complete the sentences. Use *have* or *has*.

1. I ____have____ a cold.
2. She _____ a fever.
3. You _____ a broken arm.
4. I _____ a sore throat.
5. You _____ a headache.
6. He _____ a cough.

Check your answers. See page 135.

3 Answer the questions.

1. **A** What's wrong?

   B _He has a broken arm._

2. **A** What's wrong?

   B _____

3. **A** What's wrong?

   B _____

4. **A** What's wrong?

   B _____

5. **A** What's wrong?

   B _____

6. **A** What's wrong?

   B _____

4 Write a conversation. Use the sentences in the box. Then listen.

TRACK 15

Speaker A	Speaker B
What's the matter?	I have a fever.
Take aspirin.	Not so good.
How are you?	OK. Thanks.

1. **A** _How are you?_ _____

2. **B** _____

3. **A** _____

4. **B** _____

5. **A** _____

6. **B** _____

Check your answers. See page 135.

LESSON C Do you have a cold?

Study the chart on page 129.

1 Circle the correct answers.

1. What's wrong?
   a. My daughter has a fever.
   b. My daughter have a fever.

2. Does she have a backache?
   a. No, she doesn't.
   b. No, she don't.

3. Does she have an earache?
   a. Yes, she do.
   b. Yes, she does.

4. Does she have a sore throat?
   a. No, she don't.
   b. No, she doesn't.

5. Do you have a stomachache?
   a. No, I don't.
   b. No, I do.

6. Do you have a headache?
   a. Yes, I does.
   b. Yes, I do.

2 Complete the conversation.

A Kenji is sick.

B Does he have the flu?

A Yes, he ____does____ .

B Does he have a sore throat?

A Yes, he _____ .

B Does he have a cough?

A No, he _____ .

B Does he have a fever?

A No, he _____ .

B Do you have aspirin?

A Yes, I _____ .

B How about you? Do you have the flu, too?

A No, I _____ .

B Good! Well, I hope Kenji feels better soon.

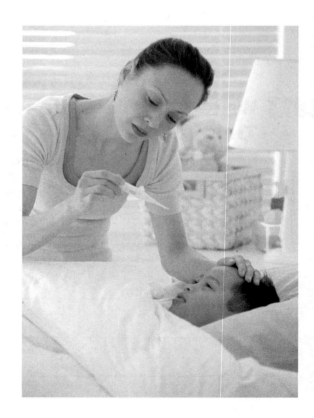

Check your answers. See page 135.

3 Write questions.

1. a stomachache

   A *Does she have a stomachache?*

   B No, she doesn't. She has a headache.

2. a sore throat

   A _____

   B Yes, he does.

3. a broken leg

   A _____

   B No, he doesn't. He has a sore ankle.

4. cold

   A _____

   B No, she doesn't. She has a sore throat.

5. a cough

   A _____

   B No, I don't. I have a sore throat.

6. a fever

   A _____

   B Yes, I do.

7. an earache

   A _____

   B Yes, she does.

8. a cut

   A _____

   B No, I don't. I have the flu.

9. a sprained ankle

   A _____

   B No, she doesn't. She has a broken leg.

10. a headache

    A _____

    B Yes, I do.

Check your answers. See page 135.

LESSON D Reading

1 **Unscramble the letters. Write the words.**

1. eot ___toe___
2. neso _____
3. lekan _____
4. yee _____

5. nich _____
6. nahd _____
7. iregnf _____
8. otof _____

9. ekne _____
10. tohot _____
11. rea _____
12. stmchao _____

2 **Complete the sentences. Use the words from Exercise 1.**

1. His ___eye___ hurts.

2. Her _____ hurts.

3. His _____ hurts.

4. His _____ hurts.

5. Her _____ hurts.

6. Her _____ hurts.

Check your answers. See page 135.

3 Number the sentences in the correct order. Then write the conversation below.

_____ Hi, Ms. Jones. I'm not so good.

_____ Thank you.

_____ My knee hurts. I have a cut.

__1__ Good morning, Jamie. How are you today?

_____ I'm sorry. Here. Use this bandage.

_____ What's wrong?

Ms. Jones _Good morning, Jamie. How are you today?_

Jamie _____

Ms. Jones _____

Jamie _____

Ms. Jones _____

Jamie _____

4 Read and answer the questions. Then listen.

TRACK 16

> Mr. Simon and his children are at the doctor's office. His 12-year-old son, Bobby, has a sore arm. His six-year-old daughter, Margaret, has a cold and a sore throat. His baby girl has a fever and a cough. Mr. Simon is tired!

1. Where are Mr. Simon and his children?

   Mr. Simon and his children are at the doctor's office.

2. What's the matter with Bobby?

   _____

3. What's wrong with Margaret?

   _____

4. Does the baby have a fever?

   _____

5. How is Mr. Simon feeling?

   _____

Check your answers. See page 135.

LESSON E Writing

1 Look at the note. Circle the items.

(October 4, 2013)

Dear Mr. Rodriguez,

Sarah Johnson is my daughter. She isn't in school today. She is at home. She has a sore throat and a fever.

Please excuse her. Thank you.

Sincerely,

Rita Johnson

1. the date
2. the teacher's name
3. the name of the sick child
4. what's wrong
5. the signature

2 Correct the note. Add capital letters.

April 14, 2013

Dear ms. nguyen,

debra garcia is my niece. she isn't in school today. she is at home. she has a cold and a fever.

please excuse her. thank you.

Sincerely,

Rob Garcia

Check your answers. See page 135.

3 **Write about Jim. He is sick, too. Complete the note.**

Dear   headache   home   nephew

October 4, 2013

_____ Ms. Nguyen,

Jim Garcia is my _____. He is sick. He has a _____. He is at _____.

Please excuse him. Thank you.

Sincerely,

Rob Garcia

4 **Number the parts of the letter in the correct order. Then write the note.**

_____ Sincerely,

Sean Jones

_____ He has a fever and a cough.

_1_ January 21, 2013

_____ Barry Jones is my son. He isn't in school today.

_____ Dear Ms. Adams,

_____ He is at home.

_____ Please excuse him. Thank you.

_____ ,

_____

_____

_____

_____

_____ ,

_____

LESSON F Another view

1 Look at the appointment card. Answer the questions.

APPOINTMENT CONFIRMATION

FOOT and ANKLE CLINIC
1875 Pacific Coast Highway

Patient: Soon-mi Won
Medical Record Number: 123456789
Date/Time: Wednesday, August 1, at 3:45 p.m.
Doctor: Jack Murphy, MD
Location: Foot and Ankle Clinic, 1875 Pacific Coast Highway

CANCELLATION INFORMATION:
To cancel only: (562) 555-4924 (7 days / 24 hours)
To cancel and reschedule: (562) 555-2034 (Mon-Fri 8:00 a.m.-4:30 p.m.)

1. What is the patient's name? _Soon-mi Won_

2. When is the appointment? _____

3. What is the doctor's name? _____

4. Where is the clinic? _____

5. What number do you call to cancel an appointment? _____

6. What number do you call to reschedule an appointment? _____

2 Complete the sentences.

cough	fever	sore throat
earache	headache	stomachache

1. He isn't eating. He has a ____stomachache____.

2. She is taking cough drops. She has a _____.

3. The teacher isn't talking today. He has a _____.

4. I'm taking aspirin. I'm hot. I have a _____.

5. My head hurts. I have a _____.

6. My ear hurts. I have an _____.

Check your answers. See page 135.

3 Look at the pictures. Complete the conversations.

1.

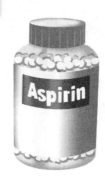

2.

3.

4.

5.

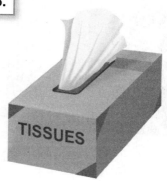

6.

1. **A** I have a headache.

   B You _____ *need aspirin* _____.

2. **A** Manuel _____ a cough.

   B He needs cough drops.

3. **A** Claudia has a backache.

   B She _____.

4. **A** I _____ a cut.

   B You need bandages.

5. **A** Do you have a cold?

   B Yes, I do. I _____.

6. **A** Lara _____ an earache.

   B She needs ear drops.

Check your answers. See page 135.

LESSON **A** Listening

1 **Write the places.**

| bus stop | hospital | pharmacy | restaurant |

1. Eat here: _restaurant_

2. See a doctor here: _____

3. Get the bus here: _____

4. Buy medicine here: _____

2 **Complete the sentences.**

| grocery store | hospital | library | museum |

1. The _____ _museum_ _____ has paintings.

2. My grandmother is sick. She is in the _____.

3. We read books at the _____.

4. We're buying groceries at the _____.

Check your answers. See page 135.

3 Listen. Then circle the correct letters.

TRACK 17

1. a.    b.

2. a.    b.

3. a.    b.

4. a.    b.

5. a.    b.

Check your answers. See page 135.

LESSON B It's on the corner.

1 Look at the map. Complete the sentences.

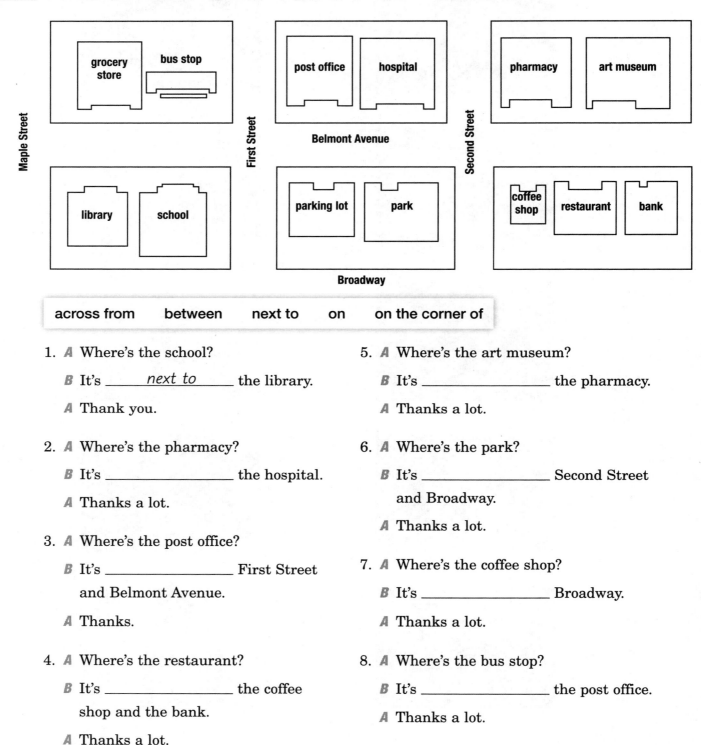

across from	between	next to	on	on the corner of

1. **A** Where's the school?

   B It's _____next to_____ the library.

   A Thank you.

2. **A** Where's the pharmacy?

   B It's _____ the hospital.

   A Thanks a lot.

3. **A** Where's the post office?

   B It's _____ First Street
   and Belmont Avenue.

   A Thanks.

4. **A** Where's the restaurant?

   B It's _____ the coffee
   shop and the bank.

   A Thanks a lot.

5. **A** Where's the art museum?

   B It's _____ the pharmacy.

   A Thanks a lot.

6. **A** Where's the park?

   B It's _____ Second Street
   and Broadway.

   A Thanks a lot.

7. **A** Where's the coffee shop?

   B It's _____ Broadway.

   A Thanks a lot.

8. **A** Where's the bus stop?

   B It's _____ the post office.

   A Thanks a lot.

Check your answers. See page 135.

2 Look at the map in Exercise 1. Answer the questions.

1. Where's the pharmacy?

   It's on the corner of Belmont Avenue and Second Street.

   (on the corner of)

2. Where's the art museum?

   _____

   (on)

3. Where's the post office?

   _____

   (next to)

4. Where's the hospital?

   _____

   (on the corner of)

5. Where's the school?

   _____

   (next to)

6. Where's the bank?

   _____

   (on)

7. Where's the bus stop?

   _____

   (next to)

8. Where's the restaurant?

   _____

   (between)

9. Where's the grocery store?

   _____

   (on the corner of)

10. Where's the library?

    _____

    (across from)

3 Look at the map in Exercise 1. Write questions.

1. _Where's the school?_   It's next to the library.
2. _____ It's on Belmont Avenue, next to the post office.
3. _____ It's on Broadway, next to the park.
4. _____ It's across from the school.
5. _____ It's on the corner of Maple Street and Broadway.
6. _____ It's next to the pharmacy.
7. _____ It's across from the library.
8. _____ It's on Belmont Avenue, between the coffee shop and the bank.

Check your answers. See pages 135–136.

LESSON C Go two blocks.

1 **Look at the map. Complete the sentences.**

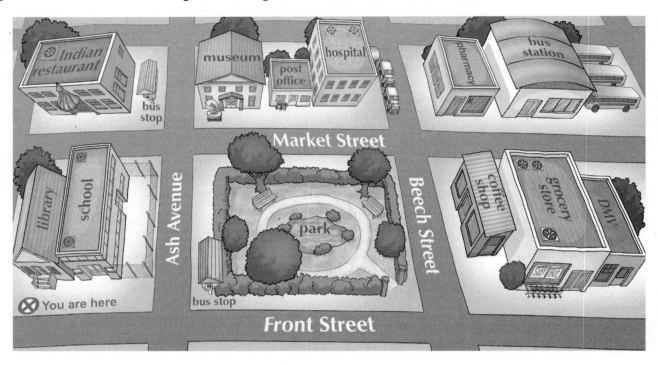

1. Go straight on Front Street. Turn left on Ash Avenue. Turn right on Market Street.
   Go straight. The ___post office___ is between the museum and the hospital.

2. Go straight on Front Street. Turn left on Ash Avenue. Turn right on Market Street.
   Go straight. The _____ is on the corner of Beech Street and Market Street.
   It's next to the post office.

3. Go straight on Front Street. Cross Ash Avenue, and cross Beech Street.
   The _____ is on the left, between the coffee shop and the DMV.

4. Go straight two blocks on Front Street. Turn left on Beech Street. Turn right on Market
   Street. The _____ is on the left, next to the pharmacy.

5. Go straight two blocks on Front Street. The _____ is on the left, on the corner
   of Beech and Front Streets. It's across from the coffee shop.

6. Go straight for one block. Turn left on Ash Avenue. Go straight for a block and a half.
   The _____ is on the left, next to the restaurant. It's across from the museum.

Check your answers. See page 136.

2 Read the directions. Look at the map in Exercise 1. Write the places.

1. Go straight two blocks on Front Street. It's on the corner of Front and Beech Streets, next to the grocery store.

   coffee shop

2. Go straight on Front Street. Turn left on Ash Avenue. Go one block. Turn left on Market Street. It's next to the bus stop.

   _____

3. Go straight on Front Street. Turn left on Ash Avenue. Turn right on Market Street. It's on your left, between the museum and the hospital.

   _____

4. Go straight two blocks on Front Street. Turn left on Beech Street. Turn right on Market Street. It's next to the pharmacy.

   _____

5. Go straight on Front Street. Turn left on Ash Avenue. Go one block. Turn right on Market Street. Go straight. It's on the corner of Market and Beech Streets.

   _____

6. Go straight on Front Street. Turn left on Ash Avenue. Go one block. Turn right on Market Street. It's on your left, across from the park.

   _____

7. Go straight on Front Street. Cross Ash Avenue. It's on your left, next to the bus stop.

   _____

LESSON D Reading

1 Complete the chart.

coffee shop	grocery store	playground	restaurant
day-care center	hospital	police station	school

Places for children	Places for food	Places for help
day-care center		

2 Complete the sentences.

apartment building	day-care center	high school	senior center	shopping mall

1. Cesar lives in a big ___apartment building___ next to the school.

2. Mrs. Won is teaching at the _____ now.

3. The _____ has many different stores.

4. Stella is taking her grandmother to the _____ today.

5. Katia is driving her three-year-old son to the _____.

3 Write a conversation. Use the sentences in the box.

Speaker A	Speaker B
The corner of Sixth and Union?	It's on the corner of Fifth and Union.
Excuse me, where's the post office?	Yes, it's next to the bank.
OK, Fifth and Union. Is it next to the bank?	No, on Fifth and Union.

1. A _Excuse me, where's the post office?_ _____

2. B _____

3. A _____

4. B _____

5. A _____

6. B _____

Check your answers. See page 136.

4 Read and answer the questions. Then listen.

TRACK 18

January 14, 2013

Dear Mary Ann,

   How are you? I'm having a great time in Los Angeles! Right now, I'm eating lunch at a Mexican restaurant and writing postcards. I want to buy stamps at the post office and visit the museum. The post office is about five blocks from the restaurant. It's next to the museum.

See you soon!
Rafael

Mary Ann Rogers
17 West Street
El Paso, TX 79910

1. Where is Rafael? <u>*He's in Los Angeles.*</u>

2. What is he doing now? _____

3. Who is Rafael writing to? _____

4. Where's the post office? _____

5. Where's the museum? _____

5 Read and answer the questions. Then listen.

TRACK 19

Hi Susan,

   I love my new apartment. It's across from my children's school. There's also a grocery store next to it. My husband works there. He walks to work. There's an Italian restaurant on the corner of Maple Street and Pine Street. It's very good. I like it here, but I miss you. Please write.

Your friend,
Hui

1. Where is Hui's apartment? <u>*It's across from her children's school.*</u>

2. Where is the grocery store? _____

3. How does Hui's husband get to work? _____

4. Is the Italian restaurant good? _____

Check your answers. See page 136.

LESSON E Writing

1 Write sentences.

1. the train station / Where's / ?

   Where's the train station? _____

2. on the corner of / The grocery store / Broadway and Main / is /.

   _____

3. the shopping mall / get to / How / I / do / ?

   _____

4. next to / the train station / is / The park /.

   _____

5. left / on / Maple Street / Turn /.

   _____

2 Complete the conversations. Use the sentences from Exercise 1.

1. **A** How do I get to the post office?

   B _Turn left on Maple Street._ _____

2. **A** Where's the grocery store?

   B _____

   _____

3. **A** _____

   B The train station is on Fifth Avenue.

4. **A** _____

   _____

   B Go straight two blocks. The shopping mall is on Grant Street.

5. **A** Where's the park?

   B _____

   _____

Check your answers. See page 136.

3 Add capital letters.

>   Janet lives at 3725 D̲elta S̲treet. She goes to school at madison adult school. She walks down delta street for three blocks and turns right on skyline drive. She goes two blocks and turns left on national avenue. The school is at 3500 national avenue, next to Bandini Bakery.

4 Correct the sentences.

1. Tina lives at Main Street.

   Tina lives on Main Street.

2. There is a library in the restaurant and the bank.

   _____

3. Go straight Main Street.

   _____

4. It's next in the school.

   _____

5. Turn left Main Street.

   _____

6. The coffee shop is across the school.

   _____

5 Complete the paragraph.

       Dr. Singh works at Mercy Hospital. Mercy Hospital is _____*between*_____ a
                                                          1. between / on

park and a shopping mall. He also teaches at Jefferson College. Jefferson College is

_____ from Jefferson Courthouse. He drives down Main Street for
   2. across / between

ten blocks and _____ left on Memorial Drive. He goes five blocks and
                    3. cross / turns

_____ right _____ Jefferson Avenue. Jefferson College is
  4. goes to / turns   5. between / on

at 2600 Jefferson Avenue, _____ Jefferson Avenue and Madison Street.
             6. across / on the corner of

Check your answers. See page 136.

1 **Read the questions. Look at the shopping mall directory. Fill in the correct answers.**

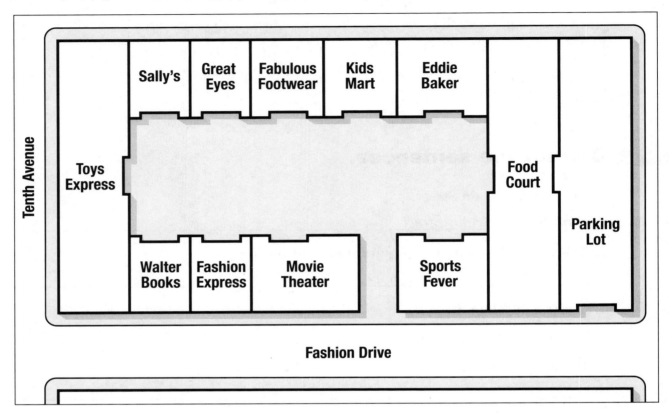

1. Where's Sports Fever?
   Ⓐ next to Fashion Express
   Ⓑ across from Great Eyes
   Ⓒ between Eddie Baker and the Food Court
   ● across from the movie theater

2. Where's Walter Books?
   Ⓐ across from Sally's
   Ⓑ next to Sally's
   Ⓒ between Sally's and Fashion Express
   Ⓓ near the Food Court

3. Where's the Food Court?
   Ⓐ on Tenth Avenue and Fashion Drive
   Ⓑ next to Great Eyes
   Ⓒ across from Kids Mart
   Ⓓ next to the parking lot

4. What's across from Great Eyes?
   Ⓐ Fashion Express
   Ⓑ Sports Fever
   Ⓒ Fabulous Footwear
   Ⓓ Eddie Baker

5. What's on the corner of Fashion Drive and Tenth Avenue?
   Ⓐ a parking lot
   Ⓑ the Food Court
   Ⓒ Toys Express
   Ⓓ Kids Mart

6. What's next to Great Eyes?
   Ⓐ Fashion Express
   Ⓑ Sally's
   Ⓒ Walter Books
   Ⓓ Tenth Avenue

Check your answers. See page 136.

2 Complete the puzzle.

| bank | DMV | hospital | house | library | museum | park | school |

Down

1. Children play at the _____.
3. The _____ has books.
5. The _____ has paintings.

Across

2. The teacher works at the _____.
4. You get a driver's license at the _____.
6. The _____ has money.
7. Dr. Ngyuen works at the _____.
8. She lives in a _____.

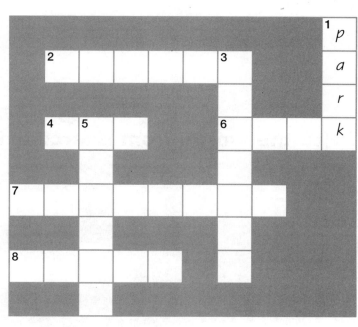

3 What do the signs say? Complete the sentences.

 1. _____Don't turn left_____ here.

 2. _____ here.

 3. _____ here.

 4. _____ here.

 5. _____ here.

LESSON **A** Listening

1 **Match the words.**

1. take ___c___   a. home
2. read _____   b. for work
3. leave _____   c. a break
4. catch _____   d. the bus
5. buy _____   e. a schedule
6. get _____   f. a snack

2 **Look at the pictures. Write the words from Exercise 1.**

1. _take a break_   2. _____   3. _____

4. _____   5. _____   6. _____

Check your answers. See page 136.

3 Listen to the conversations. Then match the activities with the times.

TRACK 20

1. take a break   _b_   a. 10:50
2. catch the bus   ____   b. 10:15
3. start work   ____   c. 2:30
4. leave for work   ____   d. 12:30
5. eat lunch   ____   e. 2:15
6. get home   ____   f. 10:45

4 Look at the clocks. Write the times in numbers.

1. ___12:00___   2. _____   3. _____   4. _____

5. _____   6. _____   7. _____   8. _____

5 Look at the clocks. Write the times in words.

eleven fifty-five	one thirty-five	six-ten	twelve-oh-five
nine-fifty	seven-fifteen	ten-forty	two twenty-five

1. ___six-ten___   2. _____   3. _____   4. _____

5. _____   6. _____   7. _____   8. _____

Check your answers. See page 136.

LESSON B What do you do in the evening?

Study the chart on page 128.

1 Complete the sentences.

1. **A** What _____ do _____ you do on Friday evening?
   (do / does)

   B I _____ go _____ to the library and _____.
   (go / goes)   (study / studies)

2. **A** What _____ your brother do on Friday evening?
   (do / does)

   B He _____ soccer.
   (play / plays)

3. **A** What does your husband do on Saturday morning?

   B He _____ shopping.
   (go / goes)

4. **A** What _____ your sister do on Saturday night?
   (do / does)

   B She _____ TV.
   (watch / watches)

5. **A** What do your sons do on Sunday?

   B They _____ and _____.
   (read / reads)   (exercise / exercises)

2 Write a conversation. Use the sentences in the box.

Speaker A	Speaker B
What do you do at night?	It's at the Washington Community School.
Where's your class?	I usually go to class.
Do you study English?	Yes, I do.

1. **A** _What do you do at night?_ _____

2. **B** _____

3. **A** _____

4. **B** _____

5. **A** _____

6. **B** _____

Check your answers. See page 136.

3 Complete the sentences.

| exercises | listen | study | watches | work |

1. **A** What do you do in the afternoon?

   B I ____study____ English.

2. **A** What does she do in the evening?

   B She _____ TV.

3. **A** What does he do in the morning?

   B He _____ .

4. **A** What do you do on Saturday night?

   B I _____ to music.

5. **A** What do they do on Sunday afternoon?

   B They _____ in the garden.

4 Write questions.

1. morning   **A** _What do you do in the morning?_____

   B I play soccer.

2. evening   **A** _____

   B I pay bills.

3. afternoon   **A** _____

   B I go shopping.

4. Saturday   **A** _____

   B I go to the park.

Check your answers. See page 136.

LESSON C I go to work at 8:00.

Study the chart on page 128.

1 Complete the chart.

eight-thirty	June	night
eleven	Monday	Thursday afternoon
the evening	the morning	Wednesday night

at	in	on
eight-thirty		

2 Read Christina's calendar. Complete the sentences. Use *at*, *in*, or *on*.

Christina's Calendar

Sunday	Monday	Tuesday	Wednesday	Thursday	Friday	Saturday
1 10:00 a.m. English class	**2** 9:00 a.m. volunteer	**3** 10:00 a.m. English class	**4** 1:00 p.m. work	**5** 10:00 a.m. English class	**6** 11:00 a.m. work	
7 7:00 p.m. Malik's birthday party!	**8** 10:00 a.m. English class	**9** 7:30 p.m. PTA meeting	**10** 10:00 a.m. English class	**11** 1:00 p.m. work	**12** 10:00 a.m. English class	**13** 11:00 a.m. work

1. **A** What time does Christina volunteer on Tuesday the 2nd?

   B She volunteers ___*at*___ 9:00 a.m.

2. **A** When is Malik's birthday party?

   B It's _____ 7:00 p.m. _____ Sunday.

3. **A** When does the PTA meeting start?

   B It starts _____ 7:30 _____ the evening _____ Tuesday the 9th.

4. **A** When does Christina work?

   B She starts _____ 1:00 p.m. _____ Thursdays and _____ 11:00 a.m. _____ Saturdays.

Check your answers. See page 137.

3 Look at the bulletin board. Answer the questions.

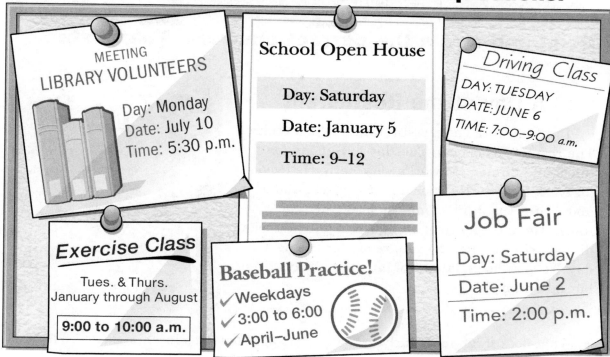

1. What time is the Library Volunteers' meeting?

   The meeting is at 5:30 p.m.

2. What day is the school open house?

   _____

3. What time does the driving class start?

   _____

4. What time does the exercise class end?

   _____

5. What day is the job fair?

   _____

6. When does the job fair start?

   _____

7. What time does baseball practice end?

   _____

8. What date is the school open house?

   _____

Check your answers. See page 137.

LESSON D Reading

1 Read and circle the correct answers. Then listen.

A Day at the Restaurant

Ibrahim works at a restaurant. He is a cook. The restaurant is open Tuesday to Sunday for lunch and dinner. He works very hard. He leaves for work early in the morning. He checks the food and writes the day's menu. At 11:00, he cooks lunch. He takes a break at 3:00. At 5:00, he cooks dinner. After dinner, he gets ready for the next day. He gets home late at night. He's always tired, but he's happy!

1. What does Ibrahim do early in the morning?
   a. He cooks lunch.
   b. He goes home.
   c. He leaves for work.
   d. He takes a break.

2. What does Ibrahim do at 11:00?
   a. He cooks lunch.
   b. He gets home.
   c. He leaves for work.
   d. He writes the menu.

3. What does Ibrahim do at 3:00?
   a. He cooks lunch.
   b. He leaves for work.
   c. He cooks dinner.
   d. He takes a break.

4. How does Ibrahim feel at night?
   a. He feels sad and tired.
   b. He feels sore but happy.
   c. He feels tired and sad.
   d. He feels tired but happy.

2 Answer the questions. Use the story in Exercise 1.

1. Where does Ibrahim work?

   He works at a restaurant.

2. When does he leave for work?

   _____

3. What does he do at 5:00?

   _____

4. When does he get home?

   _____

Check your answers. See page 137.

3 Complete the chart.

a break	dinner	a shower
breakfast	lunch	to bed
the children to school	shopping	to work

eat	go	take
breakfast		

4 Complete the sentences. Use the words from Exercise 3.

1. **A** When do they ___eat lunch___?

   B *They eat lunch at 12 o'clock.*

2. **A** When do they _____?

   B _____

3. **A** When does he _____?

   B _____

4. **A** When does she _____?

   B _____

LESSON E Writing

1 **Write questions.**

1. volunteer / does / When / she / ?

   When does she volunteer?

2. to work / she / go / does / What time / ?

   _____

3. on the weekend / do / What / you / do / ?

   _____

4. to the park / go / he / on Saturday morning / Does / ?

   _____

5. go to bed / your / What time / children / do / ?

   _____

6. does / the dog / walk / he / When / ?

   _____

2 **Complete the conversations. Use the questions from Exercise 1.**

1. *A* *When does she volunteer?* _____

   B She volunteers in the evening.

2. *A* _____

   B He walks the dog in the evening.

3. *A* _____

   B I work at a shopping mall on the weekend.

4. *A* _____

   B They go to bed at 9:00 p.m.

5. *A* _____

   B She goes to work at 8:00 a.m.

6. *A* _____

   B Yes, he does.

Check your answers. See page 137.

3 Add capital letters. Then rewrite the sentences.

1. ~~s~~usie works at the library, and she goes to school.
   S

2. she works on monday, wednesday, and friday.

3. she begins work at 9:00 a.m.

4. she has lunch from 12:00 to 1:00 p.m.

5. she finishes work at 5:00 p.m.

6. on tuesday and thursday, she doesn't work. she goes to school.

Susie works at the library, and she goes to school.

_____

_____

_____

_____

4 Complete the e-mail. Use *at*, *in*, or *on*. Then listen.

TRACK 22

To:	msmith@cup.org
From:	hamidq@cup.org
Date:	April 13, 2013
Re:	Daily Schedule

Hi Marisol,

My daily schedule isn't hard. ___*On*___ Monday, I usually get up _____ 7:00
                    1.   2.
_____ the morning. _____ 8:00, I leave for work. I eat lunch late _____
   3.   4.   5.
the afternoon because I am so busy. I leave for home _____ 6:00 _____ the
                                                   6.   7.
evening. This is my schedule Tuesday to Friday, too. _____ Saturday, I go to my
                                                         8.
friend's house. _____ Sunday morning, I spend time with my wife and children.
                      9.

Hamid

1 **Read the questions. Look at the class schedule. Fill in the correct answers.**

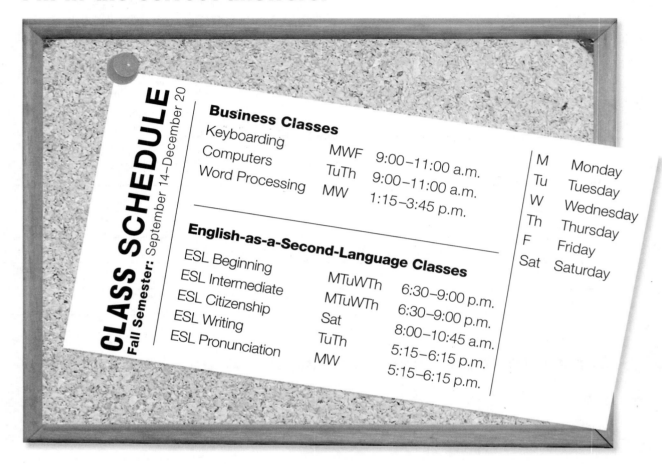

1. What semester is this schedule for?
   ● fall
   Ⓑ summer
   Ⓒ spring
   Ⓓ winter

2. When does the semester begin?
   Ⓐ September 14
   Ⓑ September 20
   Ⓒ December 14
   Ⓓ December 20

3. When does the semester end?
   Ⓐ September 14
   Ⓑ September 20
   Ⓒ December 14
   Ⓓ December 20

4. What class meets on Saturday?
   Ⓐ Computers
   Ⓑ ESL Citizenship
   Ⓒ ESL Writing
   Ⓓ ESL Pronunciation

5. When are the computer classes?
   Ⓐ Monday, Wednesday, and Friday
   Ⓑ Monday and Wednesday
   Ⓒ Tuesday and Thursday
   Ⓓ Saturday

6. When are the Beginning ESL classes?
   Ⓐ in the morning
   Ⓑ on the weekend
   Ⓒ in the afternoon
   Ⓓ in the evening

Check your answers. See page 137.

2 Look at the bold word. Cross out the choice that is different.

1. **read**   a book   ~~a movie~~   a newspaper
2. **listen to**   music   a newspaper   the radio
3. **go to**   work   the park   homework
4. **play**   baseball   TV   soccer
5. **take**   a soccer game a class   the bus

3 Look at the schedule. Complete the sentences with the correct word.

Bay City
Community Center

Hours:
8:00 a.m. – 9:00 p.m.,
Monday to Saturday

Films on Friday
A new movie every week!
This week: *Cowboys in Space*
Show time: 7:00 p.m. – 9:00 p.m.

Painting Class
Beginners welcome!
Saturdays 9:00 a.m. – 10:00 a.m.

Book Club Meeting
Wednesdays 10:00 a.m. – 12:00 noon

Community Café
Lunch – Dinner – Coffee
Hours: 12:00 noon – 7:00 p.m.,
Monday to Saturday

1. What time does the community center _____*open*_____?
   (open / start)

2. The center _____ at 9:00 p.m.
   (ends / closes)

3. The movie _____ at 7:00 p.m.
   (opens / starts)

4. What time does the class _____?
   (end / close)

5. The book club meeting _____ at 12:00 noon.
   (closes / ends)

6. The café _____ at 12:00 noon.
   (starts / opens)

LESSON **A** Listening

1 **Complete the words.**

1. ap _p_ l _e_ s

2. b ____ n ____ n ____ s

3. bre ____ ____

4. ch ____ e ____ e

5. c ____ ____ kies

6. ____ i ____ k

7. on ____ o ____ s

8. ____ ota ____ oes

9. to ____ at ____ es

2 **Look at the pictures. Write the words from Exercise 1.**

1. _milk_

2. _____

3. _____

4. _____

5. _____

6. _____

7. _____

8. _____

9. _____

Check your answers. See page 137.

3 **List the items in Exercise 2 from the lowest price (99¢) to the highest price ($4.00).**

1. _bananas_ _99¢_   4. _____ _____   7. _____ _____

2. _____ _____   5. _____ _____   8. _____ _____

3. _____ _____   6. _____ _____   9. _cheese_ _$4.00_

4 **Match the words with the numbers.**

1. five dollars and fifty-nine cents   _d_   a. $3.19

2. three dollars and ninety-nine cents   ____   b. $16.09

3. nine dollars and eleven cents   ____   c. $4.69

4. twenty dollars and twenty-five cents   ____   d. $5.59

5. twelve dollars and thirty-five cents   ____   e. $9.11

6. four dollars and sixty-nine cents   ____   f. $10.49

7. three dollars and nineteen cents   ____   g. $12.35

8. sixteen dollars and nine cents   ____   h. $3.99

9. ten dollars and forty-nine cents   ____   i. $60.09

10. sixty dollars and nine cents   ____   j. $20.25

5 **Listen to the conversations. Then circle the correct prices.**

TRACK 23

1. $1.99 $2.99   ($1.29)

2. $.99 $1.99 $.49

3. $2.59 $3.59 $2.49

4. $.99 $2.99 $1.99

5. $2.49 $2.99 $5.99

6. $2.60 $2.15 $2.50

LESSON B How many? How much?

1 **Complete the chart.**

apples	cheese	eggs	milk	peaches	rice	sugar
bananas	coffee	juice	oranges	pies	strawberries	water

How many . . . ?	How much . . . ?
apples	cheese

2 **Write questions. Use _How many_ or _How much_.**

1. **A** _How many apples do you need?_

   B I need a lot of apples.

2. **A** _____

   B She needs a lot of sugar.

3. **A** _____

   B They need a lot of strawberries.

4. **A** _____

   B You need a lot of eggs.

5. **A** _____

   B He needs a lot of water.

6. **A** _____

   B I need a lot of oranges.

Check your answers. See page 137.

3 Write a conversation. Use the sentences in the box.

Speaker A	Speaker B
We need five or six.	OK. How many apples?
Not much.	OK. See you later.
We need apples and juice.	To the grocery store.
Where are you going?	And how much juice do we need?

1. A _Where are you going?_
2. B _____
3. A _____
4. B _____
5. A _____
6. B _____
7. A _____
8. B _____

4 Complete the sentences.

a lot	many	need
does	much	needs

1. How ____much____ milk does he need?

2. We _____ a lot of meat.

3. He doesn't need _____ bananas.

4. She _____ five eggs.

5. I need _____ of apples.

6. How many peaches _____ she need?

Check your answers. See page 137.

LESSON C Are there any bananas?

1 Look at the picture. Answer the questions.

1. **A** Are there any bananas?

   B _Yes, there are._

2. **A** Is there any coffee?

   B _No, there isn't._

3. **A** Are there any blueberries?

   B _____

4. **A** Is there any bread?

   B _____

5. **A** Are there any pies?

   B _____

6. **A** Is there a pineapple?

   B _____

7. **A** Are there any eggs?

   B _____

8. **A** Is there any tea?

   B _____

9. **A** Is there any apple juice?

   B _____

10. **A** Is there any water?

    B _____

2 Unscramble the letters. Write the food containers.

1. two ___*bags*___ of rice
   (agsb)

2. a _____ of orange juice
   (tlbeto)

3. six _____ of soda
   (sacn)

4. a _____ of tea
   (obx)

5. a _____ of water
   (gslsa)

6. two _____ of milk
   (toncars)

7. a _____ of bread
   (fola)

8. a _____ of cookies
   (pagecka)

Check your answers. See pages 137–138.

3 Complete the charts. Write the singular form.

	Singular	Plural
1.	*box*	boxes
2.		cartons
3.		bottles
4.		glasses

	Singular	Plural
5.		packages
6.		cans
7.		bags
8.		loaves

4 Read the sign. Circle the correct answers.

> **Sam's Break Stand**
>
> Coffee $2.50/cup   Tea $1.99/cup
> Soda $1.00/can   Water $2.00/bottle
> Milk $1.99/carton   Juice $1.50/box

1. How much is one cup of coffee?
   a. $1.00
   b. $1.50
   c. $2.00
   (d.) $2.50

2. How much are a box of juice and a carton of milk?
   a. $2.50
   b. $4.50
   c. $3.49
   d. $4.49

3. How much is a cup of tea?
   a. one dollar and fifty-nine cents
   b. two dollars and ninety-nine cents
   c. one dollar and ninety-nine cents
   d. one dollar and fifty cents

4. How much is a bottle of water?
   a. two fifty
   b. two dollars
   c. one-twenty-five
   d. one-fifty

5 Complete the sentences. Use *There is* or *There are*.

1. _____*There are*_____ three boxes of tea.

2. _____ a carton of milk.

3. _____ a bottle of water.

4. _____ six bottles of juice.

5. _____ two packages of meat.

6. _____ twelve cans of soda.

7. _____ one bag of flour.

8. _____ a carton of eggs.

LESSON D Reading

1 Find the words.

ATM	card	credit	dollar	nickel	quarter
bill	check	dime	half	penny	

q	u	a	r	t	e	r	i	c
e	e	t	d	i	m	e	i	a
n	i	m	o	n	m	t	c	h
l	h	c	l	i	c	e	i	a
a	t	h	l	c	a	h	c	l
b	d	e	a	k	r	b	a	f
k	t	c	r	e	d	i	t	i
y	c	k	l	l	f	l	n	e
p	e	n	n	y	r	l	c	n

2 Complete the questions.

dime	five	one	quarter	ten	twenty

1. **A** Do you have change for a ___quarter___ ?

   B Sure. Here are five nickels.

2. **A** Do you have change for a _____ -dollar bill?

   B Sure. Here are four quarters.

3. **A** Do you have change for a _____ -dollar bill?

   B Sure. Here are 2 ten-dollar bills.

4. **A** Do you have change for a _____?

   B Sure. Here are two nickels.

5. **A** Do you have change for a _____ -dollar bill?

   B Sure. Here are 5 one-dollar bills.

6. **A** Do you have change for a _____ -dollar bill?

   B Sure. Here are 2 five-dollar bills.

Check your answers. See page 138.

3 Complete the sentences. Then listen.

TRACK 24

| bread | grocery | milk | onions | rice | tea |

Karima usually goes to the _____*grocery*_____ store on Thursday
1.
afternoon. Today she is shopping at Best Food Market. She is buying

a loaf of _____ , a gallon of _____ , a box
2. 3.
of _____ , a bag of _____ , and two
4. 5.
_____ . The total is $15.36. Karima only has a ten-dollar
6.
bill, but it's not a problem. She is writing a check.

4 Answer the questions about Karima. Use the information from Exercise 3.

1. What does Karima usually do on Thursday afternoon?
   She usually goes to the grocery store.

2. Where is she shopping today?
   _____

3. How much milk is she buying?
   _____

4. How much rice is she buying?
   _____

5. How many onions is she buying?
   _____

6. How much is the total?
   _____

7. How much money does she have?
   _____

8. What is she writing?
   _____

LESSON E Writing

1 Write questions.

1. we / Do / of milk / need / a carton / ?
   Do we need a carton of milk?

2. the refrigerator / juice / there / any / Is / in / ?
   _____

3. she / a bottle / Is / buying / of water / ?
   _____

4. on the shelf / Are / any / there / bananas / ?
   _____

5. How much / do / you / coffee / need / ?
   _____

6. there / oranges / How many / are / on the table / ?
   _____

7. have / you / How much / do / money / ?
   _____

8. favorite grocery store / is / What / his / ?
   _____

2 Complete the sentences.

bag	box	carton	credit card	loaf	three

James,

Please buy some groceries. We need a ____carton____ of
                                          1.
milk, _____ onions, a _____ of tea, a
            2.   3.
_____ of rice, and a _____ of bread.
       4.   5.
When you pay, use the _____ .
                            6.

Thanks,
Meg

Check your answers. See page 138.

3 Look at the picture. Complete the sentences.

1. Julie is buying a ___package___ of cookies.
2. She is buying a _____ of coffee.
3. She is buying a _____ of onions.
4. She is buying a _____ of milk.
5. She is buying a _____ of meat.
6. She is buying a _____ of tea.
7. She is buying _____ tomatoes.
8. She is buying _____ pineapple.

4 Add capital letters and commas.

      W
~~w~~alter is a regular customer at Happy Day Supermarket. he usually goes three times
a week. everybody knows him. today he's buying three apples two oranges a package of
cookies and a can of soda. he needs to pay $8.95. walter only has a five-dollar bill a
one-dollar bill and a quarter. it's not a problem. He's using his debit card.

5 Rewrite the paragraph in Exercise 4. Change *Walter* to *I*. Then listen.

TRACK 25

I am a regular customer at Happy Day Supermarket.

_____

_____

_____

_____

_____

_____

LESSON F Another view

| are | bill | card | check | half | many | nickel |
| banana | bottle | change | groceries | is | much | |

Across

1. How ____ juice do we need?
3. ____ of ten dollars is five dollars.
7. She buys ____ every week.
8. ____ there any cookies on the shelf?
9. Walter is writing a ____ at the supermarket.
10. How ____ oranges do we need?
11. I need a ____ of orange juice.
12. I have a credit ____ .

Down

2. Do you have ____ for a dollar?
4. There are five pennies in a ____ .
5. ____ there any more coffee?
6. A ____ is yellow.
11. She only has a five-dollar ____ .

Check your answers. See page 138.

2 Look at the refrigerator. Complete the conversations with *some* or *any*.

1. **A** Do we need apples?

   B No, we don't. *We have some apples.*

2. **A** Do we need bread?

   B Yes, we do. *We don't have any bread.*

3. **A** Do we need meat?

   B Yes, we do. _____

4. **A** Do we need milk?

   B No, we don't. _____

5. **A** Do we need eggs?

   B No, we don't. _____

6. **A** Do we need oranges?

   B Yes, we do. _____

7. **A** Do we need carrots?

   B No, we don't. _____

8. **A** Do we need water?

   B No, we don't. _____

9. **A** Do we need cheese?

   B Yes, we do. _____

10. **A** Do we need orange juice?

    B No, we don't. _____

Check your answers. See page 138.

LESSON **A** Listening

1 **Unscramble the letters. Write the words.**

1. rensubspo _____busperson_____
2. koco _____
3. senur _____
4. cletirenaci _____

5. verres _____
6. torcod _____
7. sngiunr natsissta _____
8. shcaier _____

2 **Where do people work? Use words from Exercise 1.**

1. restaurant _____busperson_____ _____

_____ _____

2. hospital _____ _____ _____

3 **Match the occupations with the pictures.**

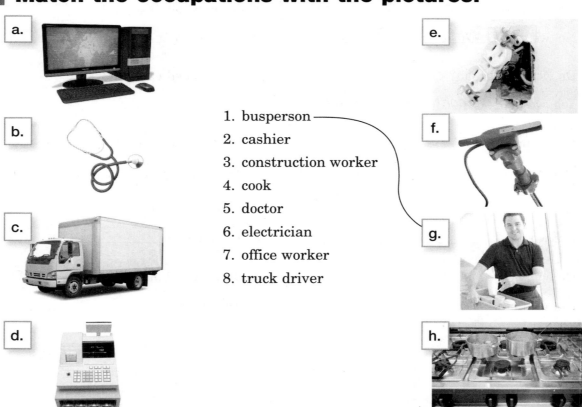

1. busperson
2. cashier
3. construction worker
4. cook
5. doctor
6. electrician
7. office worker
8. truck driver

a.

b.

c.

d.

e.

f.

g.

h.

Check your answers. See page 138.

4 Listen. Then complete the sentences with when the person worked.

TRACK 26

1.

Raphael was a busperson from ___January___ to ___June___.

2.

Imelda was a nursing assistant from _____ to _____.

3.

Ying-che was an office worker for _____ years.

4.

Roberto was a construction worker from _____ to _____.

5.

Luisa was a truck driver in _____.

6.

Petra was a cook from _____ to _____.

Check your answers. See page 138.

LESSON B I was a teacher.

Study the chart on page 129.

1 Complete the sentences. Use *am*, *are*, *is*, *was*, or *were*.

	Before		Now	
1.	She ____was____ a nurse.		She ____is____ a student.	
2.	He _____ an office worker.		He _____ a manager.	
3.	They _____ electricians.		They _____ construction workers.	
4.	I _____ a teacher.		I _____ a student.	
5.	She _____ a student.		She _____ a homemaker.	
6.	They _____ servers.		They _____ cashiers.	
7.	He _____ a nursing assistant.		He _____ a doctor.	
8.	He _____ a truck driver.		He _____ a cook.	

2 Complete the conversations. Use the correct form of *be*. Then listen.

TRACK 27

1. *A* What does Gregory do?

   B He works in a school.
   He ____is____ a teacher.

   A Really? _____ he a teacher before in his country?

   B Yes, he _____ .

2. *A* Where does Anita work?

   B She works in a bank.
   She _____ a manager.

   A Really? _____ she a manager before in her country?

   B No, she _____ .
   She _____ a teacher.

Check your answers. See page 138.

3 Write questions.

1. servers

   A *Were they servers before?*

   B No, they weren't. They were office workers.

2. teacher

   A _____

   B No, she wasn't. She was a nurse.

3. electricians

   A _____

   B No, they weren't. They were construction workers.

4. manager

   A _____

   B No, she wasn't. She was a teacher.

5. nurse

   A _____

   B No, he wasn't. He was a doctor.

4 Answer the questions. Use *No*.

1. manager

   A Was he a cashier before?

   B *No, he wasn't. He was a manager.*

2. server

   A Was he a busperson before?

   B _____

3. nurse

   A Were you a doctor before?

   B _____

4. cook

   A Was she a homemaker before?

   B _____

5. students

   A Were they teachers before?

   B _____

Check your answers. See page 138.

LESSON C Can you cook?

Study the chart on page 131.

1 Look at the chart. Answer the questions.

	Drive a truck	Work with computers	Paint	Fix a car	Speak Spanish
Mary				✓	✓
Daniel	✓		✓	✓	
Vera		✓			✓
Brenda	✓	✓			

1. Can Daniel drive a truck?   _Yes, he can._

2. Can Brenda speak Spanish? _____

3. Can Brenda and Vera paint? _____

4. Can Mary and Vera speak Spanish? _____

5. Can Daniel work with computers? _____

6. Can Mary fix a car? _____

2 Read the job ads. Match the names in Exercise 1 with the jobs.

Office Worker Needed. Can you work with computers? Speak Spanish? Then call today! 555-7797

Part-Time Driver Needed. Can you drive a truck? Can you work with computers? Must have office experience, too. Call Mondays 555-3606

Painter Needed. Can you paint? Drive a truck? We can train you on the job. Call now! 555-1234

Auto Mechanic Needed. Can you fix a car? Speak Spanish? Call us! 555-0602

1. _____Vera_____   2. _____   3. _____   4. _____

Check your answers. See pages 138–139.

3 Look at the picture. Write questions and answers.

1. cook

   A _Can he cook_____ now?

   B _No, he can't._____

2. drive

   A _____ now?

   B _____

3. speak

   A _____ now?

   B _____

4. work with a computer

   A _____ now?

   B _____

4 Answer the questions.

build things	fix cars	take care of children
drive a truck	paint	take care of plants

1. Esther is a painter. What can she do?

   _She can paint._____

2. Van is a child-care worker. What can he do?

   _____

3. Toan and Mai are auto mechanics. What can they do?

   _____

4. Abe is a truck driver. What can he do?

   _____

5. Samuel is a gardener. What can he do?

   _____

6. Terry is a carpenter. What can she do?

   _____

Check your answers. See page 139.

LESSON D Reading

1 Find the words.

factory	hotel	restaurant
home	office	school
hospital	pharmacy	store

f	r	p	h	a	r	m	a	c	y
a	e	o	h	o	p	s	c	l	d
t	s	u	o	h	o	t	e	l	a
o	t	r	s	c	h	o	o	l	u
f	a	t	p	l	o	r	f	s	r
f	u	r	i	f	m	e	f	h	s
a	r	u	t	e	e	r	i	r	m
c	a	o	a	o	m	o	c	r	o
h	n	m	l	t	h	u	e	m	n
o	t	f	a	c	t	o	r	y	e
o	h	o	p	r	e	h	o	m	l

2 Complete the sentences. Use the words from Exercise 1.

1. A housekeeper works in a _____*hotel*_____.

2. A pharmacy technician works in a _____.

3. A nurse works in a _____.

4. A homemaker works at _____.

5. A server works in a _____.

6. A salesperson works in a _____.

7. A factory worker works in a _____.

8. An office worker works in an _____.

9. A teacher works in a _____.

Check your answers. See page 139.

3 Write a conversation. Use the sentences in the box.

Speaker A	Speaker B
Hi, Francisco. What job are you looking for?	My name is Francisco.
OK. What can you do?	I can sell things. I can talk to customers.
Hello. What's your name?	I'm looking for a job as a salesperson.

1. **A** _Hello. What's your name?_ _____

2. **B** _____

3. **A** _____

4. **B** _____

5. **A** _____

6. **B** _____

4 Read and answer the questions. Then listen.

TRACK 28

> Francisco is looking for a job as a salesperson. He was a salesperson in his country. Now he's a busperson. He wants to find a job as a salesperson in this country. Francisco has many skills. He can sell things in a store. He can talk to customers. He can speak three languages.

1. Is Francisco looking for a job?

   Yes, he is. _____

2. What was Francisco's job in his country?

   _____

3. What is Francisco's job now?

   _____

4. What job does Francisco want?

   _____

5. What are Francisco's skills?

   _____

6. Can he speak more than one language?

   _____

Check your answers. See page 139.   **UNIT 8 97**

LESSON E Writing

1 Make questions.

1. work with / computers / she / Can / ?

   Can she work with computers?

2. a nurse / country / she / her / Was / in / ?

   _____

3. his / Was / in / a server / he / country / ?

   _____

4. a car / he / fix / Can / ?

   _____

5. looking for / a job / Ana / Is / ?

   _____

6. skills / are / your / What / ?

   _____

2 Complete the conversations. Use *can*, *can't*, *is*, or *was*.

1. **A** __Can__ she work with computers?

   B Yes, she _____.

2. **A** _____ he a server now?

   B No, he _____ a server in his country.

3. **A** _____ they type and write reports?

   B No, they _____.

4. **A** _____ she an office worker now?

   B Yes, she _____.

5. **A** _____ he sell things?

   B No, he _____.

6. **A** _____ she a nurse before?

   B Yes, she _____.

3 Correct the sentences.

I ____wrok____ at the Market Street Deli. It is a
 work
 1.
small __retsaraunt__ in Dallas. I am a ____servre____.
 2.   3.
I was a __nebpursos__. I can ____coko____, too. I want
 4.   5.
to be a __mangaer__.
 6.

98 UNIT 8   Check your answers. See page 139.

4 Correct the sentences. Then rewrite them.

1. Five years ago, Ana ~~is~~ *was* a manager in her country.

   Five years ago, Ana was a manager in her country.

2. Now she was a cashier.

   _____

3. She can using a cash register.

   _____

4. She can count money and talks to customers.

   _____

5. Ana and her husband likes their jobs in this country.

   _____

6. Before they are managers. Now they has new jobs.

   _____

5 Read and rewrite the paragraph. Use *was, were, wasn't,* or *weren't*. Then listen.

TRACK 29

Tonight at Pizza Palace

Jim is at Pizza Palace tonight. His boss is there, too. Jim is very busy. There are many customers in the restaurant. They aren't happy because their food isn't ready. The customers are angry. They are very hungry. Jim is hungry, too. He's also tired. Jim is ready to go home!

Last Saturday at Pizza Palace

Jim was at Pizza Palace last Saturday.

_____

_____

_____

_____

Check your answers. See page 139.

LESSON F Another view

1 Look at the job application. Answer the questions.

Employment Application

Name Gloria Fuentes	**Soc. Sec. No.** 000-99-5554
Address 2733 Beech Street, Apt. 5 Miami, Florida 74354	**Phone** (305) 555-2306
Are you 16 years or older? Yes ✓ No __	**Position desired** nursing assistant

Employment history (List most recent job first.)

Dates (from – to)	Employer name and address	Position
2012–present	Manor Inn Nursing Home 645 Palm Avenue, Miami, FL	nursing assistant
2009–2012	Family Fun Restaurant 3566 South 45th Street, Miami, FL	cashier

Important: Show your Social Security card at the time you present this application.

1. Is Gloria working now? _Yes, she is._____

2. What is Gloria's job? _____

3. Was she a nursing assistant before? _____

4. Where does she work? _____

5. Is she looking for a job? _____

6. When was she a cashier? _____

2 Complete the chart.

Skill	
cleans rooms	sells things
cuts hair	takes care of children
serves food	works with computers

Place of work	
beauty salon	office
day-care center	restaurant
hotel	store

	Occupation	Skill	Place of work
1.	child-care worker	takes care of children	day-care center
2.	hairstylist		
3.	housekeeper		
4.	office worker		
5.	salesperson		
6.	server		

Check your answers. See page 139.

3 **Read each sentence. Write two more sentences. Use the words from Exercise 2.**

		Place	**Skill**
1.	Gina is a housekeeper.	*She works in a hotel.*	*She cleans rooms.*
2.	Tim is a server.	_____	_____
3.	Carol is a salesperson.	_____	_____
4.	Tom is an office worker.	_____	_____
5.	John is a hairstylist.	_____	_____
6.	Al is a child-care worker.	_____	_____

4 **Listen and complete the sentences with *is*, *isn't*, *was*, or *wasn't*.**

TRACK 30

1. Carlos _____*isn't*_____ at work today, but he _____*was*_____ at work yesterday.

2. Lara _____ at work today, and she _____ at work yesterday.

3. Wei _____ at work today, but he _____ at work yesterday.

4. Florence _____ at work this week, but she _____ at work last week.

5. Abdi _____ at work this week, and he _____ at work last week.

6. Rob _____ at work today, but he _____ at work yesterday.

Check your answers. See page 139.

LESSON **A** Listening

1 **Unscramble the letters. Write the words.**

1. rion ___iron___
2. rloof _____
3. opm _____
4. secthol _____
5. eancl _____

6. ashtr _____
7. uumcav _____
8. obotrahm _____
9. pytme _____
10. urg _____

2 **Listen and write the number of the conversation.**

TRACK 31

Dan __1__

Alicia ____

Ana ____

Ron ____

Mary ____

Check your answers. See page 139.

3 Match the words.

1. clean _b_
2. empty ____
3. iron ____
4. mop ____
5. pay ____
6. vacuum ____

a. clothes
b. the kitchen
c. the bills
d. the floor
e. the rug
f. the trash

4 Complete the sentences.

1. She's ironing _____clothes_____.
   (dishes / clothes)

2. He's mopping the _____.
   (clothes / floor)

3. I emptied the _____.
   (wastebasket / house)

4. She vacuumed the _____.
   (rug / clothes)

5. We paid the _____.
   (bills / trash)

6. They're ironing _____.
   (dresses / bills)

7. He paid the _____.
   (ticket / clothes)

8. She emptied the _____.
   (iron / trash)

5 Read the advertisement. Answer the questions.

1. How much is the vacuum cleaner?
   _$149.99_

2. What is the company's name?
   _____

3. What is the company's phone number?
   _____

4. What city is the company in?
   _____

5. What state is the company in?

   _____

Super Vacuum Cleaner

X2R

The best vacuum cleaner ever!
Only $149.99!
Buy one today!
Sale until May 3rd!

AV
Acme Vacuums
of Cincinnati, Ohio

(514) 555-8976

Check your answers. See page 139.

LESSON B I cleaned the living room.

Study the chart on page 130.

1 Write the simple past of each verb.

1. clean   _cleaned_
2. cook   _____
3. dry   _____
4. dust   _____

5. empty   _____
6. iron   _____
7. mop   _____
8. vacuum   _____

2 Look at the pictures. Write the words from Exercise 1.

1. _____cleaned_____

2. _____

3. _____

4. _____

5. _____

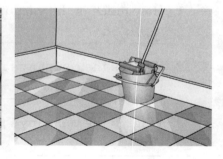

6. _____

7. _____

8. _____

Check your answers. See page 139.

3 Complete the conversations. Use the simple past *did* or *didn't*. Then listen.

TRACK 32

1. **A** _____Did_____ he wash the dishes?

   B No, he _____didn't_____.

   He _____mopped_____ the floor.
   (mop)

2. **A** _____ he dust the furniture?

   B No, he _____.

   He _____ the rug.
   (vacuum)

3. **A** _____ they cook the dinner?

   B Yes, they _____.

   They also _____ the dishes.
   (dry)

4. **A** _____ she clean her bedroom?

   B No, she _____.

   She _____ the kitchen.
   (clean)

5. **A** _____ she iron clothes?

   B No, she _____.

   She _____ the trash.
   (empty)

6. **A** _____ she dry the dishes?

   B No, she _____.

   She _____ the dishes.
   (wash)

7. **A** _____ she mop the floor?

   B No, she _____.

   She _____ the living room.
   (dust)

8. **A** _____ he clean his apartment?

   B No, he _____.

   He _____ his family's house.
   (clean)

Check your answers. See page 140.

LESSON C I paid the bills.

Study the chart on page 130.

1 Look at the picture. Write the simple past of the verbs.

do	get	make	pay

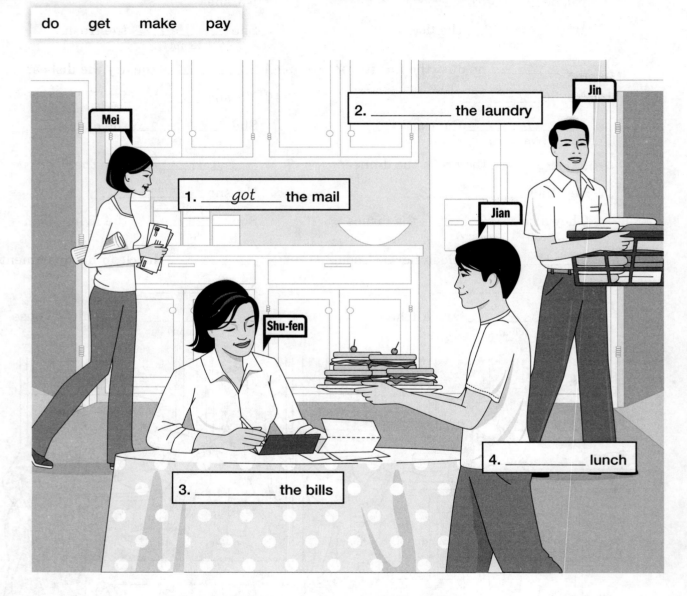

Mei

2. _____ the laundry

Jin

1. ____*got*____ the mail

Jian

Shu-fen

4. _____ lunch

3. _____ the bills

2 Complete the sentences. Use the verbs from Exercise 1.

1. **A** Who _____*got*_____ the mail?

   B *Mei did.* _____

2. **A** Who _____ lunch?

   B _____

3. **A** Who _____ the laundry?

   B _____

4. **A** Who _____ the bills?

   B _____

Check your answers. See page 140.

3 **Look at the picture. Write the simple past of the verbs.**

buy   get   make   sweep

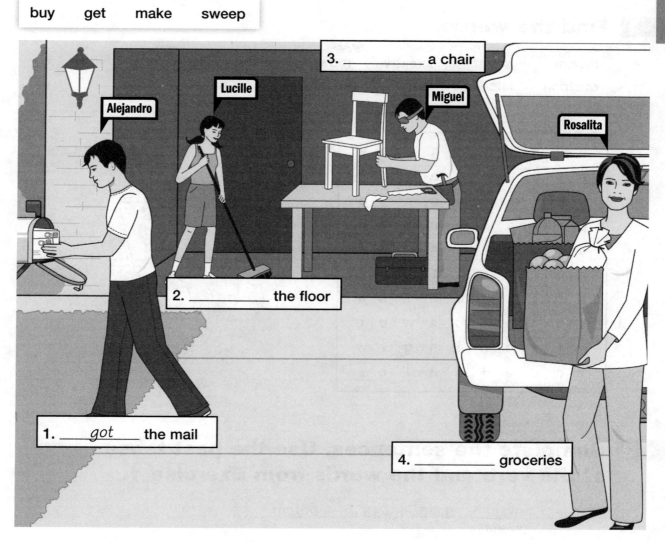

3. _____ a chair

Lucille

Alejandro

Miguel

Rosalita

2. _____ the floor

1. ___*got*___ the mail

4. _____ groceries

4 **Complete the sentences. Use *did* or *didn't* and the verbs from Exercise 3.**

1. **A** Did Lucille buy groceries?

   B No, she ___*didn't*___. She ___*swept*___ the floor.

2. **A** What did Alejandro do?

   B He _____ the mail.

3. **A** Did Miguel make a chair?

   B Yes, he _____ .

4. **A** Did Miguel buy groceries?

   B No, he _____ . He _____ a chair.

5. **A** What did Rosalita do?

   B She _____ groceries.

6. **A** Did Alejandro get the mail?

   B Yes, he _____ .

Check your answers. See page 140.

LESSON D Reading

1 Find the words.

broom	iron	laundry	mower	stove
dustpan	kitchen	mail	sponge	vacuum

```
o  w  k  i  t  c  h  e  n  y
s  t  o  v  e  f  o  o  d  v
s  b  l  a  u  n  d  r  y  e
p  r  v  a  c  u  u  m  m  u
o  o  g  p  a  s  s  u  m  g
n  o  n  y  e  v  t  k  o  b
g  m  a  i  l  d  p  i  w  a
e  n  u  a  r  b  a  w  e  t
m  i  r  o  n  i  n  g  r  w
z  c  d  e  f  n  q  i  o  s
```

2 Complete the sentences. Use the past tense of the verb and the words from Exercise 1.

1. She ____swept____ the floor with a ____broom____ .
   (sweep)

2. He _____ soup on the _____ .
   (make)

3. She _____ the grass with the lawn _____ .
   (cut)

4. She _____ the dishes with a _____ .
   (wash)

5. They _____ the rug with a _____ cleaner.
   (clean)

6. Frank _____ the _____ from the mailbox.
   (get)

Check your answers. See page 140.

3 **Read. Underline the people. Circle the chores. Then listen.**

TRACK 33

Family Chores

The <u>Cabrera family</u> (cleaned their house) last Saturday. Mom swept the kitchen. Dad mopped the kitchen floor. He also cut the grass with the lawn mower. Dad and Yolanda washed the dishes. Roberto vacuumed the rugs in the living room. He and Sara made the beds. Sara emptied the trash and got the mail. After they finished the chores, they had dinner and watched a movie.

4 **Who did each chore? Use the information from Exercise 3.**

	MOM	DAD	YOLANDA	ROBERTO	SARA
1. cut the grass		✓			
2. emptied the trash					
3. got the mail					
4. made the beds					
5. mopped the floor					
6. swept the kitchen					
7. washed the dishes					
8. vacuumed the rugs					

5 **Answer the questions.**

1. Did the Cabrera family clean their house on Sunday?

   No, they didn't. They cleaned it on Saturday.

2. Who cut the grass?

3. Who made the beds?

4. Who swept the kitchen?

5. Did Yolanda get the mail?

Check your answers. See page 140.

LESSON E Writing

1 Read the chore chart. Then answer the questions.

PERSON	CHORE	COMPLETED?
Jason	pay the bills	✓
Samantha	do the laundry	
Linda	vacuum the rug	✓
Jordan	make the beds	✓
John	sweep the kitchen	
Chantelle	make dinner	✓

1. Who paid the bills?

   Jason paid the bills.

2. Did Samantha do the laundry?

   _____

3. Who made the beds?

   _____

4. Did Chantelle make dinner?

   _____

5. Who vacuumed the rug?

   _____

6. Did John sweep the kitchen?

   _____

7. Did Jason vacuum the rug?

   _____

8. Did Jordan make dinner?

   _____

Check your answers. See page 140.

2 Complete the sentences.

| bathroom | chores | grass | laundry | rug | weekend |
| bills | floor | groceries | mail | trash | works |

Every ___weekend___, the Johnson family does _____.
　　　　　　1.　　　　　　　　　　　　　　　　　　　2.
Lucille buys _____. Vince cuts the _____. Lynn cleans
　　　　　　　3.　　　　　　　　　　　　　4.
the _____ and sweeps the _____. Nicky gets the
　　　5.　　　　　　　　　　　　　6.
_____ and pays the _____. Ida empties the _____.
　7.　　　　　　　　　　　8.　　　　　　　　　　　　　9.
Raymond does the _____ and vacuums the _____.
　　　　　　　　　　10.　　　　　　　　　　　　11.
Everyone _____ very hard.
　　　　　12.

3 Rewrite the paragraph from Exercise 2. Use the simple past.

Last weekend, the Johnson family did chores.

_____

_____

_____

_____

_____

_____

_____

_____

1 Look at the chart. Fill in the correct answers.

Student	Erase the whiteboard	Help new students	Turn off lights and lock doors	Get class books	Put away books
RAS			RIVERVIEW **ADULT SCHOOL:** Tuesday's Classroom Duties		
Andrei	✓				
Soon-yi		✓			
Hector				✓	
Marjane			✓		
Salvatore					✓

1. Who helped new students?
   Ⓐ Andrei
   ● Soon-yi
   Ⓒ Hector
   Ⓓ Salvatore

2. Who got the books?
   Ⓐ Andrei
   Ⓑ Hector
   Ⓒ Marjane
   Ⓓ Salvatore

3. Who locked the doors?
   Ⓐ Andrei
   Ⓑ Soon-yi
   Ⓒ Marjane
   Ⓓ Hector

4. Did Marjane turn off the lights?
   Ⓐ Yes, she did.
   Ⓑ No, she didn't.
   Ⓒ Marjane didn't.
   Ⓓ She checked attendance.

5. Did Andrei erase the whiteboard?
   Ⓐ Yes, I did.
   Ⓑ Yes, he did.
   Ⓒ No, he didn't.
   Ⓓ He turned off the lights.

6. Who put away the books?
   Ⓐ Andrei
   Ⓑ Soon-yi
   Ⓒ Hector
   Ⓓ Salvatore

Check your answers. See page 140.

2 **Look at the chore list. Write questions and answers about the people. Use *or*.**

Saturday Chores

Mom	do the laundry
Grandma	make dinner
Dad	mop the floor
Sam	walk the dog
Jessie	empty the trash
Annie	cut the grass

1. Mom: make dinner / do the laundry
   A _Does Mom usually make dinner or do the laundry_ on Saturday?
   B _Mom usually does the laundry._

2. Annie: make dinner / cut the grass
   A _____ on Saturday?
   B _____

3. Dad: mop the floor / cut the grass
   A _____ on Saturday?
   B _____

4. Grandma: make dinner / walk the dog
   A _____ on Saturday?
   B _____

5. Sam: empty the trash / walk the dog
   A _____ on Saturday?
   B _____

6. Jessie: empty the trash / mop the floor
   A _____ on Saturday?
   B _____

Check your answers. See page 140.

LESSON **A** Listening

1 **Find the words.**

| camping | canoeing | fishing | going on a picnic | hiking | swimming |

g	o	i	n	g	o	n	a	p	i	c	n	i	c
i	n	g	m	g	f	w	p	l	o	m	h	k	m
c	a	n	o	e	i	n	g	g	i	x	o	f	i
r	o	n	h	c	s	g	e	c	e	p	c	e	s
i	c	i	a	k	h	b	k	a	f	r	a	m	l
c	a	n	i	i	i	y	f	m	e	q	s	g	a
p	h	i	k	i	n	g	i	p	a	u	w	p	t
i	o	f	e	i	g	g	n	i	x	a	i	y	e
c	i	l	a	g	g	k	i	n	d	y	n	o	z
g	s	w	i	m	m	i	n	g	f	m	b	e	l

2 **Look and write. Use the words from Exercise 1.**

1. _____ hiking

2. _____

3. _____

4. _____

5. _____

6. _____

Check your answers. See page 140.

3 Look at the chart. Circle the correct answers.

	Canoeing	Soccer	Swimming	Camping	Fishing	Hiking
Kent Park			✓	✓	✓	✓
Palisades Park	✓	✓		✓	✓	✓
Beaver Park		✓	✓			
Daniels Park			✓			✓
City Park	✓		✓		✓	

1. Which parks have canoeing?
   a. Beaver Park and Daniels Park
   b. Palisades Park and City Park
   c. Daniels Park and Beaver Park
   d. Kent Park and Palisades Park

2. Which park has swimming and soccer?
   a. Beaver Park
   b. Daniels Park
   c. Kent Park
   d. Palisades Park

3. Which parks have fishing and hiking?
   a. Beaver Park and Palisades Park
   b. City Park and Kent Park
   c. Daniels Park and City Park
   d. Kent Park and Palisades Park

4. Which parks have fishing and swimming?
   a. Beaver Park and City Park
   b. Kent Park and City Park
   c. Daniels Park and Kent Park
   d. Palisades Park and City Park

5. Which park has canoeing and soccer?
   a. City Park
   b. Daniels Park
   c. Kent Park
   d. Palisades Park

6. Which parks have camping?
   a. Beaver Park and City Park
   b. Daniels Park and Kent Park
   c. City Park and Palisades Park
   d. Kent Park and Palisades Park

4 Listen to the conversations. Circle the words you hear.

TRACK 34

1. last weekend   (yesterday)   last week
2. last week   today   last weekend
3. last Saturday   yesterday   last night
4. last night   last Sunday   last Saturday
5. last month   last week   last weekend
6. last week   last Sunday   yesterday

Check your answers. See page 140.

LESSON B What did you do yesterday?

Study the chart on page 130.

1 Complete the simple past verbs.

1. do   d _i_ d
2. drive   dr ____ ve
3. eat   ____ te
4. go   w ____ nt
5. have   h ____ d

6. make   m ____ de
7. read   r ____ ____ d
8. see   s ____ w
9. sleep   sl ____ pt
10. write wr ____ te

2 Complete the conversations. Use words from Exercise 1.

1. A When did John _____go_____ to the hospital?

   B He _____went_____ last weekend.

2. A What did they _____ for dinner last night?

   B They _____ spaghetti.

3. A What did you _____ last weekend?

   B We _____ to the beach.

4. A Did he _____ a note to his sister?

   B Yes, he did.

5. A What did she _____ to Los Angeles last week?

   B She _____ the truck.

6. A What did you _____ at the library yesterday?

   B I _____ some newspapers.

7. A Did they _____ late last Saturday?

   B Yes, they did.

8. A Who did she _____ at school?

   B She _____ her friend.

Check your answers. See page 140.

3 **Complete the sentences. Use the simple past.**

April 7, 2013

Last week, we went on vacation. On Saturday, we _____went hiking_____. On Sunday,
                                                    1. go hiking

we _____. On Monday, we _____. On Tuesday,
       2. go on a picnic   3. go swimming

we _____. On Wednesday, we _____. On Thursday, we
       4. read books   5. sleep late

_____. On Friday night, we _____.
       6. go fishing   7. eat pizza

4 **Look at the paragraph in Exercise 3. Write questions or answers.**

1. _What did they do last week?_ _____

   They went on vacation.

2. _____

   They went hiking.

3. _____

   They went on a picnic.

4. What did they do on Monday?

   _____

5. _____

   They read books.

6. What did they do on Wednesday?

   _____

7. _____

   They went fishing.

8. What did they do on Friday night?

   _____

LESSON C What are you going to do?

Study the chart on page 131.

1 Read the Serrano family's schedule. Answer the questions.

Monday	Tuesday	Wednesday
play basketball	play soccer	buy clothes

Thursday	Friday	Saturday
go to a party	watch a movie	drive to a lake

1. What is the Serrano family going to do on Saturday?

   They are going to drive to a lake.

2. What is Mr. and Mrs. Serrano's son going to do on Tuesday?

   _____

3. What are Mr. and Mrs. Serrano going to do on Friday night?

   _____

4. What is Mr. Serrano going to do on Monday?

   _____

5. What is Mr. and Mrs. Serrano's daughter going to do on Wednesday?

   _____

6. What are Mrs. Serrano and the children going to do on Thursday?

   _____

Check your answers. See page 141.

2 Write sentences. Use *be going to*.

1. She __'s going to go__
   (go)
   fishing next weekend.

2. He _____
   (go)
   swimming this afternoon.

3. They _____
   (play)
   soccer tonight.

4. We _____
   (take)
   a trip next week.

5. I _____
   (clean)
   the house tomorrow.

6. She _____
   (buy)
   a house next year.

3 Complete the sentences.

1. **A** What's Chris going to do today?

   B He's _going to go swimming_____.
      (go swimming)

2. **A** What's Jim going to do tomorrow?

   B He's _____.
      (go shopping)

3. **A** What are Hirori and Ross going to do tonight?

   B They're _____.
      (cook dinner)

4. **A** What's Sue going to do next week?

   B She's _____.
      (take a vacation)

5. **A** What's Shane going to do today?

   B He's _____.
      (rest)

LESSON D Reading

1 **Which words go with *go* or *play*? Write the words.**

baseball	camping	football	ice hockey	soccer
basketball	fishing	hiking	skiing	swimming

go   **play**

1. _____camping_____   6. _____

2. _____   7. _____

3. _____   8. _____

4. _____   9. _____

5. _____   10. _____

2 **Complete the sentences. Use the simple past.**

Last Saturday, the Chan family ____was____ very busy. On Saturday morning, Mr. Chan
                                  1. be

_____ his family to the park. Mrs. Chan _____ a walk in the park with her
   2. drive   3. take

friend. Mr. Chan _____ his daughter, Amy, play soccer. After the game, the family
                     4. watch

_____ lunch at home. In the afternoon, they _____ some work around the
   5. eat   6. do

house. Mrs. Chan _____ tired, so she _____ a nap. Mr. Chan _____
                   7. be   8. take   9. watch

ice hockey on television. Amy _____ shopping with her friends. On Saturday night,
                                10. go

they _____ dinner at a Mexican restaurant.
       11. eat

Check your answers. See page 141.

3 Read and answer the questions about Raul's vacation. Then listen.

TRACK 35

Summer Vacation

Last summer I went camping with friends. We stayed at a campground. We went fishing in the morning. Every day we ate fish for lunch! In the afternoon, we went hiking. After hiking, we went swimming in the lake to relax. We went to bed late, and we got up early in the morning. We talked to other campers and made new friends. We had a great time.

HAPPY CAMPER CAMPGROUND

HIKING! SWIMMING! BOATING!

Open Weekends (201) 555-6978

1. What did Raul do last summer?

   He went camping with friends.

2. What did they do in the morning?

   _____

3. What did they eat for lunch?

   _____

4. What did they do in the afternoon?

   _____

5. Where did they go swimming?

   _____

6. When did they go to bed?

   _____

4 Number the sentences in the correct order.

_____ Finally, they're going to go to bed, tired but happy in their new home.

_____ In the morning, they're going to put boxes and furniture into a truck.

_____ At 6:00 p.m., they're going to go to a restaurant to celebrate.

_____ Then, they're going to drive the truck to their new house.

_____ In the afternoon, they're going to bring the boxes and furniture into their new house.

_1_ Tomorrow, the Velasco family is going to move to a new house.

Check your answers. See page 141.

LESSON E Writing

1 Write a conversation. Use the sentences in the box.

Speaker A	Speaker B
Who did you go with?	I went fishing.
What did you do last weekend?	My brother and I are going to go hiking this weekend.
What are you going to do this weekend?	I went with my brother.

1. **A** *What did you do last weekend?* _____

2. **B** _____

3. **A** _____

4. **B** _____

5. **A** _____

6. **B** _____

2 Write sentences.

1. What / last weekend / do / did / you / ?
   What did you do last weekend? _____

2. in the mountains / went hiking / We / .

   _____

3. go / Did / you / with your son / ?

   _____

4. No, / a friend / went / with / I / .

   _____

5. swimming / go / Did / you / ?

   _____

6. canoeing / Yes, / we / went swimming / and / .

   _____

7. next weekend / to do / What / you / are / going / ?

   _____

Check your answers. See page 141.

3 Read the paragraph. Add capital letters.

A
ali had a good weekend. On Saturday, he went to a

baseball game with his friend. they ate hot dogs and popcorn.

they came home at 5:00. on Sunday, ali played soccer with

his friends at the park near his house. they played all

afternoon. they had a good time.

4 Correct the sentences.

went
1. I go to the park last weekend.

2. Maria drive to the shopping mall yesterday.

3. Ali and Miriam eat Chinese food last weekend.

4. John play soccer last weekend.

5. What do you going to do next Friday?

6. Is he go to go to the concert on Sunday?

7. He ride the bus to the concert next Sunday.

5 Read and rewrite the paragraph. Change *Susanna* to *Susanna and Maria*. Then listen.

TRACK 36

Susanna is going to go camping on Saturday. She needs some food. She is going to buy some bread, milk, and eggs. Then she is going to drive to the beach. In the afternoon, she is going to go hiking. On Sunday morning, she is going to go swimming and fishing. She likes to exercise.

Susanna and Maria are going to go camping on Saturday. They _____

_____

_____

_____

_____

LESSON F Another view

1 **Look at the ad. Fill in the correct answers.**

> # SAN DIEGO CITY FAIR
> ## Del Mar Fairgrounds
> San Diego, California
> June 16–July 5
> Fireworks: July 4
> Hot-dog-eating contest: June 23
>
> Hours: 10 a.m. to 10 p.m., Sundays through Thursdays
> 10 a.m. to 11 p.m., Fridays and Saturdays
>
> Admission: Adults: $12.50
> Seniors 62 and older: $9.00
> Children 6–12: $7.00
> Children 5 and younger: free
>
> Discounts: Every Tuesday, children 12
> and younger get in free. Free parking,
> with free shuttle bus to fairgrounds.
> **Information: (858) 555-1161**

1. When does the fair start?
   ● June 16
   Ⓑ June 23
   Ⓒ July 4
   Ⓓ July 5

2. How much is a ticket for a 10-year-old on a Tuesday?
   Ⓐ $7.00
   Ⓑ $9.00
   Ⓒ $12.50
   Ⓓ It's free.

3. When is the hot-dog-eating contest?
   Ⓐ June 16
   Ⓑ June 23
   Ⓒ July 4
   Ⓓ July 5

4. When does the fair end?
   Ⓐ June 16
   Ⓑ June 24
   Ⓒ July 4
   Ⓓ July 5

5. How much is parking?
   Ⓐ $7.00
   Ⓑ $9.00
   Ⓒ $12.50
   Ⓓ It's free.

6. When does the fair close on Saturday nights?
   Ⓐ 9:00 p.m.
   Ⓑ 10:00 p.m.
   Ⓒ 11:00 p.m.
   Ⓓ midnight

Check your answers. See page 141.

2 Look at the chart. Write sentences about the people's activities.

Name	Last weekend	Next weekend	Every weekend
1. Duc	go hiking	go camping	go to the movies
2. Luis	go swimming	go fishing	play soccer
3. Claudia	go camping	go to the movies	clean her apartment
4. Lara	go on a picnic	play Ping-Pong	do the laundry
5. Ivan	go fishing	go hiking	play Ping-Pong

1. *Duc went hiking last weekend.*
   He's going to go camping next weekend.
   He goes to the movies every weekend.

2. _____

   _____

   _____

3. _____

   _____

   _____

4. _____

   _____

   _____

5. _____

   _____

   _____

Check your answers. See page 141.

Reference

Present of *be*

Affirmative statements

I'm		
You're		
He's		
She's	from Somalia.	
It's		
We're		
You're		
They're		

Negative statements

I'm		
You're		
He's		
She's	not	from Somalia.
It's		
We're		
You're		
They're		

Contractions

I'm	=	I am
You're	=	You are
He's	=	He is
She's	=	She is

It's	=	It is
We're	=	We are
You're	=	You are
They're	=	They are

Yes / No questions

Am	I	
Are	you	
Is	he	
Is	she	
Is	it	from Guatemala?
Are	we	
Are	you	
Are	they	

Short answers

	you are.	
	I am.	
	he is.	
	she is.	
Yes,	it is.	
	you are.	
	we are.	
	they are.	

	you aren't.	
	I'm not.	
	he isn't.	
	she isn't.	
No,	it isn't.	
	you aren't.	
	we aren't.	
	they aren't.	

Present continuous

Affirmative statements

I'm	
You're	
He's	
She's	eating.
It's	
We're	
You're	
They're	

Yes / No questions

Am	I	
Are	you	
Is	he	
Is	she	eating?
Is	it	
Are	we	
Are	you	
Are	they	

Short answers

	you are.	
	I am.	
	he is.	
Yes,	she is.	
	it is.	
	you are.	
	we are.	
	they are.	

	you aren't.	
	I'm not.	
	he isn't.	
No,	she isn't.	
	it isn't.	
	you aren't.	
	we aren't.	
	they aren't.	

Wh- questions

	am	I	
	are	you	
	is	he	
	is	she	
What	is	it	doing?
	are	we	
	are	you	
	are	they	

Answers

You're	
I'm	
He's	
She's	
It's	eating.
You're	
We're	
They're	

Possessive adjectives

Questions

	my	
	your	
	his	
	her	
What's	its	address?
	our	
	your	
	their	

Answers

Your	
My	
His	
Her	
Its	address is 10 Main Street.
Your	
Our	
Their	

Simple present

Affirmative statements

I	work.
You	work.
He	works.
She	works.
It	works.
We	work.
You	work.
They	work.

Negative statements

I	don't	
You	don't	
He	doesn't	
She	doesn't	
It	doesn't	work.
We	don't	
You	don't	
They	don't	

Yes / No questions

Do	I	
Do	you	
Does	he	
Does	she	
Does	it	work?
Do	we	
Do	you	
Do	they	

Short answers

	you	do.
	I	do.
	he	does.
Yes,	she	does.
	it	does.
	you	do.
	we	do.
	they	do.

	you	don't.
	I	don't.
	he	doesn't.
No,	she	doesn't.
	it	doesn't.
	you	don't.
	we	don't.
	they	don't.

Wh- questions: What

	do	I	
	do	you	
	does	he	
What	does	she	do at 7:00?
	does	it	
	do	we	
	do	you	
	do	they	

Answers

You	work.
I	work.
He	works.
She	works.
It	works.
You	work.
We	work.
They	work.

Wh- questions: When

	do	I	
	do	you	
	does	he	
When	does	she	usually work?
	does	it	
	do	we	
	do	you	
	do	they	

Answers

You	usually	work	
I			
He			
She	usually	works	on Friday.
It			
You			
We	usually	work	
They			

Simple present of *have*

Affirmative statements

I	have	
You	have	
He	has	a cold.
She	has	
We	have	
You	have	colds.
They	have	

Negative statements

I	don't have	
You	don't have	
He	doesn't have	a cold.
She	doesn't have	
We	don't have	
You	don't have	colds.
They	don't have	

Yes / No questions

Do	I	have	
Do	you	have	
Does	he	have	a cold?
Does	she	have	
Do	we	have	
Do	you	have	colds?
Do	they	have	

Short answers

	you	do.
	I	do.
	he	does.
Yes,	she	does.
	you	do.
	we	do.
	they	do.

	you	don't.
	I	don't.
	he	doesn't.
No,	she	doesn't.
	you	don't.
	we	don't.
	they	don't.

Simple past of *be*

Affirmative statements

I	was	
You	were	
He	was	a teacher.
She	was	
We	were	
You	were	teachers.
They	were	

Negative statements

I	wasn't	
You	weren't	
He	wasn't	a cashier.
She	wasn't	
We	weren't	
You	weren't	cashiers.
They	weren't	

Yes / No questions

Was	I	
Were	you	
Was	he	a teacher?
Was	she	
Were	we	
Were	you	teachers?
Were	they	

Short answers

	you	were.
	I	was.
	he	was.
Yes,	she	was.
	you	were.
	we	were.
	they	were.

	you	weren't.
	I	wasn't.
	he	wasn't.
No,	she	wasn't.
	you	weren't.
	we	weren't.
	they	weren't.

Simple past of regular and irregular verbs

Affirmative statements

I		I	
You		You	
He		He	
She	cooked.	She	slept.
It		It	
We		We	
You		You	
They		They	

Negative statements

I		
You		
He		
She	didn't	cook. / sleep.
It		
We		
You		
They		

Yes / No questions

	I	
	you	
	he	
Did	she	cook? / sleep?
	it	
	we	
	you	
	they	

Short answers

	you	
	I	
	he	
Yes,	she	did.
	it	
	you	
	we	
	they	

	you	
	I	
	he	
No,	she	didn't.
	it	
	you	
	we	
	they	

Wh- questions

		I	
		you	
		he	
What	did	she	do?
		it	
		we	
		you	
		they	

Answers

You		You	
I		I	
He		He	
She	cooked.	She	slept.
It		It	
You		You	
We		We	
They		They	

Regular verbs

Add -ed: cook → cooked   vacuum → vacuumed
          dust → dusted   wash → washed

Irregular verbs

break → broke	get → got	ride → rode	sweep → swept
buy → bought	go → went	run → ran	swim → swam
do → did	have → had	see → saw	take → took
drink → drank	make → made	sell → sold	wear → wore
drive → drove	pay → paid	sit → sat	write → wrote
eat → ate	read → read	sleep → slept	

Can

Affirmative statements

I		
You		
He		
She	can	help.
It		
We		
You		
They		

Negative statements

I		
You		
He		
She	can't	help.
It		
We		
You		
They		

Yes / No questions

	I	
	you	
	he	
Can	she	help?
	it	
	we	
	you	
	they	

Short answers

	you	
	I	
	he	
Yes,	she	can.
	it	
	you	
	we	
	they	

	you	
	I	
	he	
No,	she	can't.
	it	
	you	
	we	
	they	

Future – *be going to*

Affirmative statements

I'm		
You're		
He's		
She's	going to	play soccer.
We're		
You're		
They're		

Negative statements

I'm		
You're		
He's		
She's	not going to	play soccer.
We're		
You're		
They're		

Wh- questions

	am	I	
	are	you	
	is	he	
What	is	she	going to do tomorrow?
	is	it	
	are	we	
	are	you	
	are	they	

Answer key

Welcome

Exercise 1A page 2
Marie, Abdi, Wendy, Bao, Claudia, Carlos

Exercise 1B page 2
Women's Names: Claudia, Wendy, Marie
Men's Names: Abdi, Bao, Carlos

Exercise 2A page 3
Aa, Bb, Cc, Dd, Ee, Ff, Gg, Hh, Ii, Jj, Kk, Ll, Mm, Nn, Oo, Pp, Qq, Rr, Ss, Tt, Uu, Vv, Ww, Xx, Yy, Zz

Exercise 2B page 3
Rafael, Peter, Sachi, Flore, Asad, Lena

Exercise 3A page 4
one 1; two 2; three 3; four 4; five 5; six 6; seven 7; eight 8; nine 9; ten 10

Exercise 3B page 4
1. three
2. seven
3. one
4. five
5. four
6. nine

Exercise 4A page 5
Sunday Sun.; Monday Mon.; Tuesday Tues.; Wednesday Wed.; Thursday Thurs.; Friday Fri.; Saturday Sat.

Exercise 4B page 5
Monday, Tuesday, Friday, Saturday

Exercise 4C page 5
1. January
2. February
3. March
4. April
5. May
6. June
7. July
8. August
9. September
10. October
11. November
12. December

Unit 1:
Personal information

Lesson A: Listening

Exercise 1 page 6
1. first
2. middle
3. last
4. telephone
5. area
6. zip

Exercise 2 page 6
1. first name
2. area code
3. last name
4. telephone number
5. middle name
6. zip code

Exercise 3 page 7
1. b   3. d   5. c
2. e   4. a

Exercise 4 page 7
1. Park
2. 15 Franklin Street
3. 555-1972
4. Camille
5. 631

Exercise 5 page 7
1. (631) 555-7810
2. (642) 555-1972
3. (432) 555-9803
4. (798) 555-6421

Lesson B: What's your name?

Exercise 1 page 8
1. f   3. h   5. b   7. d
2. c   4. a   6. g   8. e

Exercise 2 page 8
1A. his   3A. her
1B. His   3B. Her
2A. his   4A. their
2B. His   4B. Their

Exercise 3 page 8
1. b   2. b   3. a

Exercise 4 page 9
1A. his   3A. their
1B. His   3B. Their
2A. her
2B. Her

Exercise 5 page 9
1. His name is John Brown-Hudson.
2. Her first name is Mary.
3. Their last name is Lopez.
4. His area code is 608.
5. Their zip code is 02455.
6. Her telephone number is 555-1234.

Lesson C: Are you from Canada?

Exercise 1 page 10
1. We're   4. She's
2. They're   5. I'm
3. He's   6. They're

Exercise 2 page 10
1. She's from Ecuador.
2. He's from China.
3. He isn't from Korea.
4. They're from Colombia.
5. You're from India.
6. They're from Mexico.
7. They aren't from Russia.
8. She isn't from Brazil.
9. You aren't from Japan.
10. She's from the United States.

Exercise 3 page 11
1. No, he isn't.
2. Yes, he is.
3. No, she isn't.
4. Yes, she is.
5. No, I'm not.
6. Yes, I am.
7. No, they aren't.
8. Yes, they are.

Exercise 4 page 11
1A. is   4A. are
1B. is   4B. are
2A. Are   5A. is
2B. am   5B. is
3A. Is   6A. is
3B. is   6B. is

Lesson D: Reading

Exercise 1 page 12

Exercise 2 page 12
1. title   6. city
2. initial   7. state
3. address   8. zip code
4. street   9. signature
5. apartment

Exercise 3 page 13

Name:
| Cabrera | Juan | Carlos |
| Last | First | Middle |

Address:
138 Clark Avenue, Apt. 6

| Tampa, | Florida | 33629 |
| City | State | Zip |

Phone:
(813) 555 - 3461

Exercise 4 page 13
1. a   3. a   5. b
2. a   4. b   6. b

Lesson E: Writing

Exercise 1 page 14
1. They are from China.
2. Where are you from?
3. Mary is her middle name.
4. My zip code is 92122.
5. How do you spell that?
6. His address is 1241 Washington Avenue.

7. What is your telephone number?
8. Their area code is 202.

Exercise 2 page 14
1. His name is Bill Jackson.
2. He is a new student.
3. His address is 371 Purdy Avenue.
4. His telephone number is 555-7819.
5. He is from New York.

Exercise 3 page 15
1. last name
2. area code
3. zip code
4. telephone number
5. address
6. middle initial

Exercise 4 page 15
1. I'm Terri.
2. Hi, Terri. What's your last name?
3. My last name is Smith.
4. OK. What's your telephone number?
5. My telephone number is
   (545) 555-7771.
6. Thanks. We'll call you soon.

Lesson F: Another view

Exercise 1 page 16
1. Sue
2. Valley Adult School
3. 91109
4. V00-82496
5. Hudson Avenue
6. L.
7. Pasadena
8. Crane
9. 4A

Exercise 2 page 16
1. A   2. C   3. B   4. C

Exercise 3 page 17
1. Her; She's; b
2. His; He's; c
3. His; He's; f
4. His; He's; d
5. Their; They're; a
6. Her; She's; e

Exercise 4 page 17
Answers will vary.

Unit 2: At school

Lesson A: Listening

Exercise 1 page 18
1. calculator   6. clock
2. book   7. desk
3. pencil   8. eraser
4. map   9. notebook
5. table   10. ruler

Exercise 2 page 18
1. clock   6. desk
2. map   7. eraser
3. book   8. ruler
4. calculator   9. pencil
5. table   10. notebook

Exercise 3 page 19
On the table: calculator, book
Under the desk: ruler, notebook
In the desk: pencil, eraser

Exercise 4 page 19
1. a   3. a   5. b
2. b   4. b

Lesson B: Where is the pen?

Exercise 1 page 20
1. computer, on
2. eraser, in
3. ruler, under
4. calendar, on
5. dictionary, under
6. calculator, in

Exercise 2 page 20
1. a   2. b   3. b   4. a

Exercise 3 page 21
1. on   3. in
2. on   4. under

Exercise 4 page 21
1A. Where's the pencil?
1B. It's on the table.
2A. Where's the eraser?
2B. It's under the table.
3A. Where's the ruler?
3B. It's in the box.
4A. Where's the clock?
4B. It's in the cabinet.

Exercise 5 page 21
3   5   1   6   4   2

Lesson C: Where are the pencils?

Exercise 1 page 22
1. cabinet   8. map
2. dictionary   9. clocks
3. notebooks   10. laptops
4. desks   11. calendar
5. erasers   12. books
6. rulers   13. table
7. pencils   14. calculator

Exercise 2 page 23
Singular nouns

cabinet	dictionary
calculator	map
calendar	table

Plural nouns

books	laptops
clocks	notebooks
desks	pencils
erasers	rulers

Exercise 3 page 23
1. they are   6. it isn't
2. it isn't   7. they are
3. they are   8. they are
4. it is   9. it isn't
5. they aren't   10. they are

Exercise 4 page 23
1A. Where are the calculators?
1B. They are on the desk.
2A. Is the book under the table?
2B. No, it isn't.

Lesson D: Reading

Exercise 1 page 24

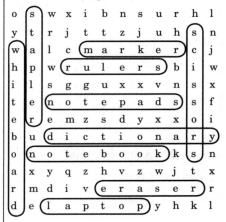

Exercise 2 page 24
1. f   3. e   5. d
2. b   4. a   6. c

Exercise 3 page 25
1. May I help you?
2. Yes, please. Where are the notebooks?
3. The notebooks are on the top shelf.
4. Thanks. I also need a pencil.
5. The pencils are on the bottom shelf.
6. Good. Now I'm ready to write!

Exercise 4 page 26
1. The notepads are in the desk drawer.
2. The stapler is on the desk.
3. The calculators are in the cabinet.
4. The pencils are in a box on the shelf.
5. The notebooks are under the calculators.
6. The erasers are in the box.

Lesson E: Writing

Exercise 1 page 26
1. Where are the books?
2. The clock is on the wall.
3. Are the books in the cabinet?
4. The pencils are on the desk.
5. Is the ruler under the notebook?
6. Where is the laptop?
7. The notebook is on the desk.
8. Is the stapler in the drawer?

Exercise 2 page 27
1. it is   5. it is
2. they aren't   6. they are
3. it is   7. it is
4. it isn't   8. it isn't

Exercise 3 page 27
1. The classroom is ready for the students.
2. The books are in the cabinet.
3. The map is on the wall.

4. The clock is on the filing cabinet.
5. The pencils are on the table.
6. The laptop is on the table.
7. The markers are in the drawer.
8. The calculators are under the desks.

Lesson F: Another view

Exercise 1 page 28

1. A   3. D   5. D   7. B
2. B   4. A   6. D   8. C

Exercise 2 page 29

1. This is   6. Those are
2. Those are   7. Those are
3. These are   8. That is
4. That is   9. This is
5. That is   10. These are

Unit 3:
Friends and family

Lesson A: Listening

Exercise 1 page 30

1. brother   4. grandfather
2. mother   5. grandmother
3. father   6. sister

Exercise 2 page 30

1. grandfather   4. brother
2. grandmother   5. mother
3. sister   6. father

Exercise 3 page 31

1. wife   4. mother
2. son   5. grandfather
3. daughter

Exercise 4 page 31

1. grandfather   4. father
2. grandmother   5. brother
3. mother

Lesson B: What are you doing?

Exercise 1 page 32

1. 's reading   5. 's watching
2. 's talking   6. 's listening
3. 's cooking   7. 're studying
4. 's eating   8. 's sleeping

Exercise 2 page 32

1. He's studying English.
2. He's reading a book.
3. He's eating lunch.
4. He's listening to music.
5. He's watching TV.

Exercise 3 page 33

is listening, is cooking, are watching, are
eating, is reading

Exercise 4 page 33

A: Hello?
B: Hi, Maria. This is Raul.
A: Oh, hi, Raul.
B: What are you doing?
A: I'm busy. I'm studying English.
B: Oh, sorry. I'll call back later.

Lesson C: Are you working now?

Exercise 1 page 34

1. Yes, he is.
2. No, she isn't.
3. No, he isn't.
4. No, he isn't.
5. Yes, she is.
6. No, they aren't.
7. No, she isn't.
8. Yes, he is.

Exercise 2 page 34

1. She is working.
2. She is listening to music.
3. He is talking on the telephone.
4. They are reading.

Exercise 3 page 34

1. Is she working?
2. Is she listening to music?
3. Is he talking on the telephone?
4. Are they reading?

Exercise 4 page 35

1. Andrea is working now.
2. Steve is driving to work.
3. Consuela is taking a break.
4. Jorge is helping Luis.
5. Amy and Nick are eating popcorn.

Lesson D: Reading

Exercise 1 page 36

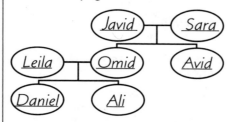

Exercise 2 page 36

1. husband
2. mother
3. wife
4. sister
5. brother
6. grandson
7. daughter
8. son
9. grandfather
10. grandmother

Exercise 3 page 37

1. grandmother
2. grandfather
3. sister-in-law
4. uncle
5. sister
6. niece
7. nephew
8. cousin

Exercise 4 page 37

a o v h k k n h z o m r l r x
m f b g g l v u z h k d g x n
z f a d k m z s y s w i f e i
o w j p o a s b i x b c j b e
f a t h e r n a l z g a o v c
q h h t h x w n g e r n n d e
u e n m w e e d h o a e u d l
r t w o d k l t h x n p a z o
a u n t z i a s m u d h v e o
n y s h q f g y n n f e c y f
i t f e d s o d f u a w i o z
x c r q i c e a m t s m k s
j o a y s u s w d a h z d e w
u r w z q b u n c l e v v s e
g r a n d m o t h e r n l c n

Lesson E: Writing

Exercise 1 page 38

1A. What are you doing?
1B. I'm cooking dinner.
2A. How many brothers do you have?
2B. I have two brothers.
3A. Do you have any sisters?
3B. Yes, I have five sisters.

Exercise 2 page 38

1. Today is Ana's birthday.
2. She is 15 years old.
3. Ana's mother, Luisa, is making a
   birthday cake.
4. Her grandparents are wrapping
   presents.
5. Ana is having a big party.
6. Her friends are dancing at the party.
7. Ana's father, Reynaldo, is taking
   pictures.
8. They are very happy today.

Exercise 3 page 39

1. We're having
2. They're talking
3. They're singing
4. She's cooking
5. He's taking

Exercise 4 page 39

1. married   5. brother
2. daughter   6. son
3. sister   7. nephew
4. single   8. cousin

Lesson F: Another view

Exercise 1 page 40

1. B   3. A   5. D
2. C   4. B   6. A

Exercise 2 page 41

1. son   5. music
2. daughter   6. TV
3. birthday   7. guitar
4. watching   8. friend

Exercise 3 page 41

1. it	4. them	7. it	
2. him	5. it	8. him	
3. her	6. them		

Unit 4: Health

Lesson A: Listening

Exercise 1 page 42

Exercise 2 page 42

Parts of the body

ankle	head
back	stomach
ear	

Problems

ache	fever
cold	sore
cough	

Exercise 3 page 42

1. c	2. d	3. a	4. b

Exercise 4 page 43

1. headache	4. sore throat
2. stomachache	5. cough
3. backache	6. fever

Exercise 5 page 43

1. a headache
2. a cough
3. a broken leg
4. a sore throat
5. an earache

Lesson B: I have a headache.

Exercise 1 page 44

1. c	2. a	3. b	4. d

Exercise 2 page 44

1. have	4. have
2. has	5. have
3. have	6. has

Exercise 3 page 45

1. He has a broken arm.
2. He/She has a cut.
3. He has a backache.
4. He has a sprained ankle.
5. He has a cold.
6. She has a stomachache.

Exercise 4 page 45

A: How are you?
B: Not so good.

A: What's the matter?
B: I have a fever.
A: Take aspirin.
B: OK. Thanks.

Lesson C: Do you have a cold?

Exercise 1 page 46

1. a	3. b	5. a
2. a	4. b	6. b

Exercise 2 page 46

does, does, doesn't, doesn't, do, don't

Exercise 3 page 47

1. Does she have a stomachache?
2. Does he have a sore throat?
3. Does he have a broken leg?
4. Does she have a cold?
5. Do you have a cough?
6. Do you have a fever?
7. Does she have an earache?
8. Do you have a cut?
9. Does she have a sprained ankle?
10. Do you have a headache?

Lesson D: Reading

Exercise 1 page 48

1. toe	7. finger
2. nose	8. foot
3. ankle	9. knee
4. eye	10. tooth
5. chin	11. ear
6. hand	12. stomach

Exercise 2 page 48

1 eye	4. stomach
2. ankle	5. knee
3. hand	6. ear

Exercise 3 page 49

2	6	4	1	5	3

Exercise 4 page 49

1. Mr. Simon and his children are at the doctor's office.
2. Bobby has a sore arm.
3. Margaret has a cold and a sore throat.
4. Yes, the baby has a fever.
5. Mr. Simon is tired!

Lesson E: Writing

Exercise 1 page 50

1. October 4, 2013
2. Mr. Rodriguez
3. Sarah Johnson
4. sore throat and a fever
5. Rita Johnson

Exercise 2 page 50

Dear Miss Nguyen,
    Debra Garcia is my niece. She isn't in school today. She is at home. She has a cold and a fever.
    Please excuse her. Thank you.
Sincerely,
Rob Garcia

Exercise 3 page 51

October 4, 2013
Dear Ms. Nguyen,
    Jim Garcia is my nephew. He is sick. He has a headache. He is at home today.
    Please excuse him. Thank you.
Sincerely,
Rob Garcia

Exercise 4 page 51

7	5	1	3	2	4	6

Lesson F: Another view

Exercise 1 page 52

1. Soon-mi Won
2. Wednesday, August 1, at 3:45 p.m.
3. Jack Murphy, MD
4. 1875 Pacific Coast Highway
5. (562) 555-4924
6. (562) 555-2034

Exercise 2 page 52

1. stomachache	4. fever
2. cough	5. headache
3. sore throat	6. earache

Exercise 3 page 53

1. need aspirin
2. has
3. needs a heating pad
4. have
5. need tissues
6. has

Unit 5: Around town

Lesson A: Listening

Exercise 1 page 54

1. restaurant	3. bus stop
2. hospital	4. pharmacy

Exercise 2 page 54

1. museum	3. library
2. hospital	4. grocery store

Exercise 3 page 55

1. b	3. a	5. a
2. a	4. b	

Lesson B: It's on the corner.

Exercise 1 page 56

1. next to
2. across from
3. on the corner of
4. between
5. next to
6. on the corner of
7. on
8. across from

Exercise 2 page 57

1. It's on the corner of Belmont Avenue and Second Street.
2. It's on Belmont Avenue.
3. It's next to the hospital.
4. It's on the corner of Belmont Avenue and Second Street.
5. It's next to the library.

6. It's on Belmont Avenue.
7. It's next to the grocery store.
8. It's between the coffee shop and the bank.
9. It's on the corner of Belmont Avenue and Maple Street.
10. It's across from the grocery store.

Exercise 3 page 57
1. Where's the school?
2. Where's the hospital?
3. Where's the parking lot?
4. Where's the bus stop?
5. Where's the library?
6. Where's the art museum?
7. Where's the grocery store?
8. Where's the restaurant?

Lesson C: Go two blocks.

Exercise 1 page 58
1. post office
2. hospital
3. grocery store
4. bus station
5. park
6. bus stop

Exercise 2 page 59
1. coffee shop
2. Indian restaurant
3. post office
4. bus station
5. hospital
6. museum
7. park

Lesson D: Reading

Exercise 1 page 60
Places for children
day-care center
school
playground
Places for food
coffee shop
grocery store
restaurant
Places for help
hospital
police station

Exercise 2 page 60
1. apartment building
2. high school
3. shopping mall
4. hospital
5. day-care center

Exercise 3 page 60
1. Excuse me, where's the post office?
2. It's on the corner of Fifth and Union.
3. The corner of Sixth and Union?
4. No, on Fifth and Union.
5. OK, Fifth and Union. Is it next to the bank?
6. Yes, it's next to the bank.

Exercise 4 page 61
1. He's in Los Angeles.
2. He's eating lunch at a Mexican restaurant and writing postcards.
3. He's writing to Mary Ann.

4. It's about five blocks from the restaurant.
5. It's next to the post office.

Exercise 5 page 61
1. It's across from her children's school.
2. It's next to Lin's apartment.
3. He walks to work.
4. Yes, it's very good.

Lesson E: Writing

Exercise 1 page 62
1. Where's the train station?
2. The grocery store is on the corner of Broadway and Main.
3. How do I get to the shopping mall?
4. The park is next to the train station.
5. Turn left on Maple Street.

Exercise 2 page 62
1. Turn left on Maple Street.
2. The grocery store is on the corner of Broadway and Main.
3. Where's the train station?
4. How do I get to the shopping mall?
5. The park is next to the train station.

Exercise 3 page 63
Janet lives at 3725 Delta Street. She goes to school at Madison Adult School. She walks down Delta Street for three blocks and turns right on Skyline Drive. She goes two blocks and turns left on National Avenue. The school is at 3500 National Avenue, next to Bandini Bakery.

Exercise 4 page 63
1. Tina lives on Main Street.
2. There is a library between the restaurant and the bank.
3. Go straight on Main Street.
4. It's next to the school.
5. Turn left on Main Street.
6. The coffee shop is across from the school.

Exercise 5 page 63
1. between
2. across
3. turns
4. turns
5. on
6. on the corner of

Lesson F: Another view

Exercise 1 page 64
1. D
2. A
3. D
4. A
5. C
6. B

Exercise 2 page 65
Down
1. park
3. library
5. museum

Across
2. school
4. DMV
6. bank
7. hospital
8. house

Exercise 3 page 65
1. Don't turn left
2. Don't fish
3. Don't use cell phones

4. Don't ride bicycles
5. Don't park

Unit 6: Time

Lesson A: Listening

Exercise 1 page 66
1. c
2. e
3. b
4. d
5. f
6. a

Exercise 2 page 66
1. take a break
2. read a schedule
3. catch the bus
4. buy a snack
5. get home
6. leave for work

Exercise 3 page 67
1. b
2. d
3. f
4. a
5. c
6. e

Exercise 4 page 67
1. 12:00
2. 8:45
3. 3:45
4. 4:20
5. 6:00
6. 8:25
7. 5:30
8. 11:00

Exercise 5 page 67
1. six-ten
2. ten-forty
3. two twenty-five
4. nine-fifty
5. twelve-oh-five
6. seven-fifteen
7. eleven fifty-five
8. one thirty-five

Lesson B: What do you do in the evening?

Exercise 1 page 68
1A. do
1B. go, study
2A. does
2B. plays
3B. goes
4A. does
4B. watches
5B. read, exercise

Exercise 2 page 68
1. What do you do at night?
2. I usually go to class.
3. Where's your class?
4. It's at the Washington Community School.
5. Do you study English?
6. Yes, I do.

Exercise 3 page 69
1. study
2. watches
3. exercises
4. listen
5. work

Exercise 4 page 69
1. What do you do in the morning?
2. What do you do in the evening?
3. What do you do in the afternoon?
4. What do you do on Saturday?

Lesson C: I go to work at 8:00.

Exercise 1 page 70

at	on
eight-thirty	Monday
eleven	Thursday afternoon
night	Wednesday night

in
the evening
June
the morning

Exercise 2 page 70
1. at
2. at, on
3. at, in, on
4. at, on, at, on

Exercise 3 page 71
1. The meeting is at 5:30 p.m.
2. It's on Saturday.
3. It starts at 7:00 a.m.
4. It ends at 10:00 a.m.
5. It's on Saturday.
6. It starts at 2:00 p.m.
7. It ends at 6:00.
8. It's on January 5.

Lesson D: Reading

Exercise 1 page 72
1. c   2. a   3. d   4. d

Exercise 2 page 72
1. He works at a restaurant.
2. He leaves for work early in the morning.
3. He cooks dinner.
4. He goes home late at night.

Exercise 3 page 73
eat
breakfast
dinner
lunch
go
shopping
to bed
to work
take
a break
the children to school
a shower

Exercise 4 page 73
1A. eat lunch
1B. They eat lunch at 12 o'clock.
2A. take a break
2B. They take a break at 3:30.
3A. go to work
3B. He goes to work at 8 o'clock.
4A. go to bed
4B. She goes to bed at 10 o'clock.

Lesson E: Writing

Exercise 1 page 74
1. When does she volunteer?
2. What time does she go to work?
3. What do you do on the weekend?
4. Does he go to the park on Saturday morning?
5. What time do your children go to bed?
6. When does he walk the dog?

Exercise 2 page 74
1. When does she volunteer?
2. When does he walk the dog?
3. What do you do on the weekend?
4. What time do your children go to bed?
5. What time does she go to work?
6. Does he go to the park on Saturday morning?

Exercise 3 page 75
1. Susie works at the library, and she goes to school.
2. She works on Monday, Wednesday, and Friday.
3. She begins work at 9:00 a.m.
4. She has lunch from 12:00 to 1:00 p.m.
5. She finishes work at 5:00 p.m.
6. On Tuesday and Thursday, she doesn't work. She goes to school.

Exercise 4 page 75
1. On   4. At   7. in
2. at   5. in   8. On
3. in   6. at   9. On

Lesson F: Another view

Exercise 1 page 76
1. A   3. D   5. C
2. A   4. D   6. D

Exercise 2 page 77
1. a movie
2. a newspaper
3. homework
4. TV
5. a soccer game

Exercise 3 page 77
1. open   4. end
2. closes   5. ends
3. starts   6. opens

Unit 7: Shopping

Lesson A: Listening

Exercise 1 page 78
1. apples   6. milk
2. bananas   7. onions
3. bread   8. potatoes
4. cheese   9. tomatoes
5. cookies

Exercise 2 page 78
1. milk   6. bananas
2. tomatoes   7. apples
3. potatoes   8. bread
4. cheese   9. onions
5. cookies

Exercise 3 page 79
1. bananas 99¢
2. bread $1.79
3. apples $1.90
4. tomatoes $2.29
5. milk $2.49
6. cookies $2.50
7. onions $2.69
8. potatoes $2.99
9. cheese $4.00

Exercise 4 page 79
1. d   5. g   9. f
2. h   6. c   10. i
3. e   7. a
4. j   8. b

Exercise 5 page 79
1. $1.29   4. $1.99
2. $.99   5. $2.49
3. $3.59   6. $2.50

Lesson B: How many? How much?

Exercise 1 page 80
How many . . . ?

apples	peaches
bananas	pies
eggs	strawberries
oranges	

How much . . . ?

cheese	rice
coffee	sugar
juice	water
milk	

Exercise 2 page 80
1. How many apples do you need?
2. How much sugar does she need?
3. How many strawberries do they need?
4. How many eggs do I need?
5. How much water does he need?
6. How many oranges do you need?

Exercise 3 page 81
1. Where are you going?
2. To the grocery store.
3. We need apples and juice.
4. OK. How many apples?
5. We need five or six.
6. And how much juice do we need?
7. Not much.
8. OK. See you later.

Exercise 4 page 81
1. much   4. needs
2. need   5. a lot
3. many   6. does

Lesson C: Are there any bananas?

Exercise 1 page 82
1. Yes, there are.
2. No, there isn't.
3. No, there aren't.
4. Yes, there is.
5. Yes, there are.
6. Yes, there is.
7. No, there aren't.
8. No, there isn't.
9. No, there isn't.
10. Yes, there is.

ANSWER KEY 137

Exercise 2 page 82

1. bags
2. bottle
3. cans
4. box
5. glass
6. cartons
7. loaf
8. package

Exercise 3 page 83

1. box
2. carton
3. bottle
4. glass
5. package
6. can
7. bag
8. loaf

Exercise 4 page 83

1. d   2. c   3. c   4. b

Exercise 5 page 83

1. There are
2. There is
3. There is
4. There are
5. There are
6. There are
7. There is
8. There is

Lesson D: Reading

Exercise 1 page 84

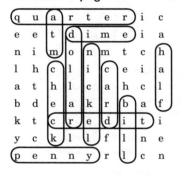

Exercise 2 page 84

1. quarter
2. one
3. twenty
4. dime
5. five
6. ten

Exercise 3 page 85

1. grocery
2. bread
3. milk
4. tea
5. rice
6. onions

Exercise 4 page 85

1. She usually goes to the grocery store.
2. She is shopping at Best Food Market.
3. She is buying a gallon of milk.
4. She is buying a bag of rice.
5. She is buying two onions.
6. The total is $15.36.
7. She has a ten-dollar bill.
8. She is writing a check.

Lesson E: Writing

Exercise 1 page 86

1. Do we need a carton of milk?
2. Is there any juice in the refrigerator?
3. Is she buying a bottle of water?
4. Are there any bananas on the shelf?
5. How much coffee do you need?
6. How many oranges are there on the table?

7. How much money do you have?
8. What is his favorite grocery store?

Exercise 2 page 86

1. carton
2. three
3. box
4. bag
5. loaf
6. credit card

Exercise 3 page 87

1. package
2. can
3. bag
4. carton
5. package
6. box
7. three
8. one

Exercise 4 page 87

Walter is a regular customer at Happy Day Supermarket. He usually goes three times a week. Everybody knows him. Today he's buying three apples, two oranges, a package of cookies, and a can of soda. He needs to pay $8.95. Walter only has a five-dollar bill, a one-dollar bill, and a quarter. It's not a problem. He's using his debit card.

Exercise 5 page 87

I am a regular customer at Happy Day Supermarket. I usually go three times a week. Everybody knows me. Today I'm buying three apples, two oranges, a package of cookies, and a can of soda. I need to pay $8.95. I only have a five-dollar bill, a one-dollar bill, and a quarter. It's not a problem. I'm using my debit card.

Lesson F: Another view

Exercise 1 page 88

Across
1. much
3. Half
7. groceries
8. Are
9. check
10. many
11. bottle
12. card

Down
2. change
4. nickel
5. Is
6. banana
11. bill

Exercise 2 page 89

1. We have some apples.
2. We don't have any bread.
3. We don't have any meat.
4. We have some milk.
5. We have some eggs.
6. We don't have any oranges.
7. We have some carrots.
8. We have some water.
9. We don't have any cheese.
10. We have some orange juice.

Unit 8: Work

Lesson A: Listening

Exercise 1 page 90

1. busperson
2. cook
3. nurse

4. electrician
5. server
6. doctor
7. nursing assistant
8. cashier

Exercise 2 page 90

1. busperson, cashier, cook, server
2. doctor, nurse, nursing assistant

Exercise 3 page 90

1. g   3. f   5. b   7. a
2. d   4. h   6. e   8. c

Exercise 4 page 91

1. January, June
2. 2009, 2012
3. 10
4. 2006, 2010
5. 2009
6. March, November

Lesson B: I was a teacher.

Exercise 1 page 92

Before
1. was
2. was
3. were
4. was
5. was
6. were
7. was
8. was

Now
1. is
2. is
3. are
4. am
5. is
6. are
7. is
8. is

Exercise 2 page 92

1B. is
1A. Was
1B. was
2B. is
2A. Was
2B. wasn't, was

Exercise 3 page 93

1. Were they servers before?
2. Was she a teacher before?
3. Were they electricians before?
4. Was she a manager before?
5. Was he a nurse before?

Exercise 4 page 93

1. No, he wasn't. He was a manager.
2. No, he wasn't. He was a server.
3. No, I wasn't. I was a nurse.
4. No, she wasn't. She was a cook.
5. No, they weren't. They were students.

Lesson C: Can you cook?

Exercise 1 page 94

1. Yes, he can.
2. No, she can't.
3. No, they can't.
4. Yes, they can.
5. No, he can't.
6. Yes, she can.

Exercise 2 page 94
1. Vera
2. Brenda
3. Daniel
4. Mary

Exercise 3 page 95
1A. Can he cook
1B. No, he can't.
2A. Can he drive
2B. No, he can't.
3A. Can he speak
3B. Yes, he can.
4A. Can he work with a computer
4B. Yes, he can.

Exercise 4 page 95
1. She can paint.
2. He can take care of children.
3. They can fix cars.
4. He can drive a truck.
5. He can take care of plants.
6. She can build things.

Lesson D: Reading

Exercise 1 page 96

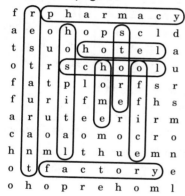

Exercise 2 page 96
1. hotel
2. pharmacy
3. hospital
4. home
5. restaurant
6. store
7. factory
8. office
9. school

Exercise 3 page 97
1. Hello. What's your name?
2. My name is Francisco.
3. Hi, Francisco. What job are you looking for?
4. I'm looking for a job as a salesperson.
5. OK. What can you do?
6. I can sell things. I can talk to customers.

Exercise 4 page 97
1. Yes, he is.
2. He was a salesperson in his country.
3. Now he's a busperson.
4. He wants to find a job as a salesperson.
5. He can sell things in a store. He can talk to customers.
6. Yes, he can speak three languages.

Lesson E: Writing

Exercise 1 page 98
1. Can she work with computers?
2. Was she a nurse in her country?
3. Was he a server in his country?
4. Can he fix a car?
5. Is Ana looking for a job?
6. What are your skills?

Exercise 2 page 98
1A. Can
1B. can
2A. Is
2B. was
3A. Can
3B. can't
4A. Is
4B. is
5A. Can
5B. can't
6A. Was
6B. was

Exercise 3 page 98
1. work
2. restaurant
3. server
4. busperson
5. cook
6. manager

Exercise 4 page 99
1. Five years ago, Ana was a manager in her country.
2. Now she is a cashier.
3. She can use a cash register.
4. She can count money and talk to customers.
5. Ana and her husband like their jobs in this country.
6. Before they were managers. Now they have new jobs.

Exercise 5 page 99
Jim was at Pizza Palace last Saturday. His boss was there, too. Jim was very busy. There were many customers in the restaurant. They weren't happy because their food wasn't ready. The customers were angry. They were very hungry. Jim was hungry, too. He was also tired. Jim was ready to go home!

Lesson F: Another view

Exercise 1 page 100
1. Yes, she is.
2. She is a nursing assistant.
3. Yes, she was.
4. She works at Manor Inn Nursing Home.
5. Yes, she is.
6. She was a cashier from 2009 to 2012.

Exercise 2 page 100
Skill
1. takes care of children
2. cuts hair
3. cleans rooms
4. works with computers
5. sells things
6. serves food

Place of work
1. day-care center
2. beauty salon
3. hotel
4. office
5. store
6. restaurant

Exercise 3 page 101
Place
1. She works in a hotel.
2. He works in a restaurant.
3. She works in a store.
4. He works in an office.
5. He works in a beauty salon.
6. He works in a day-care center.

Skill
1. She cleans rooms.
2. He serves food.
3. She sells things.
4. He works with computers.
5. He cuts hair.
6. He takes care of children.

Exercise 4 page 101
1. isn't, was
2. is, was
3. isn't, was
4. is, wasn't
5. is, was
6. is, wasn't

Unit 9: Daily living

Lesson A: Listening

Exercise 1 page 102
1. iron
2. floor
3. mop
4. clothes
5. clean
6. trash
7. vacuum
8. bathroom
9. empty
10. rug

Exercise 2 page 102
1. Dan
2. Alicia
3. Ron
4. Mary
5. Ana

Exercise 3 page 103
1. b
2. f
3. a
4. d
5. c
6. e

Exercise 4 page 103
1. clothes
2. floor
3. wastebasket
4. rug
5. bills
6. dresses
7. ticket
8. trash

Exercise 5 page 103
1. $149.99
2. Acme Vacuums
3. (514) 555-8976
4. Cincinnati
5. Ohio

Lesson B: I cleaned the living room.

Exercise 1 page 104
1. cleaned
2. cooked
3. dried
4. dusted
5. emptied
6. ironed
7. mopped
8. vacuumed

Exercise 2 page 104
1. cleaned
2. emptied
3. cooked
4. ironed
5. dusted
6. mopped
7. dried
8. vacuumed

Exercise 3 page 105

1A. Did
1B. didn't, mopped
2A. Did
2B. didn't, vacuumed
3A. Did
3B. did, dried
4A. Did
4B. didn't, cleaned
5A. Did
5B. didn't, emptied
6A. Did
6B. didn't, washed
7A. Did
7B. didn't, dusted
8A. Did
8B. didn't, cleaned

Lesson C: I paid the bills.

Exercise 1 page 106

1. got   3. paid
2. did   4. made

Exercise 2 page 106

1A. got   3A. did
1B. Mei did.   3B. Jin did.
2A. made   4A. paid
2B. Jian did.   4B. Shu-fen did.

Exercise 3 page 107

1. got   3. made
2. swept   4. bought

Exercise 4 page 107

1. didn't, swept   4. didn't, made
2. got   5. bought
3. did   6. did

Lesson D: Reading

Exercise 1 page 108

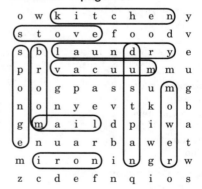

Exercise 2 page 108

1. swept, broom   4. washed, sponge
2. made, stove   5. cleaned, vacuum
3. cut, mower   6. got, mail

Exercise 3 page 109
People (underlined)

Cabrera family
Mom
Dad
Yolanda
Roberto
Sara

Chores (circled)

cleaned their house
swept the kitchen
mopped the kitchen floor
cut the grass
washed the dishes
vacuumed the rugs
made the beds
emptied the trash
got the mail

Exercise 4 page 109

1. Dad   5. Dad
2. Sara   6. Mom
3. Sara   7. Dad, Yolanda
4. Roberto, Sara   8. Roberto

Exercise 5 page 109

1. No, they didn't. They cleaned it on Saturday.
2. Dad cut the grass.
3. Sara and Roberto made the beds.
4. Mom swept the kitchen.
5. No, she didn't. Yolanda washed the dishes. / No, she didn't. Sara got the mail.

Lesson E: Writing

Exercise 1 page 110

1. Jason did.
2. No, she didn't.
3. Jordan made the beds.
4. Yes, she did.
5. Linda vacuumed the rug.
6. No, he didn't.
7. No, he didn't.
8. No, he didn't.

Exercise 2 page 111

1. weekend   7. mail
2. chores   8. bills
3. groceries   9. trash
4. grass   10. laundry
5. bathroom   11. rug
6. floor   12. works

Exercise 3 page 111

Last weekend, the Johnson family did chores. Lucille bought groceries. Vince cut the grass. Lynn cleaned the bathroom and swept the floor. Nicky got the mail and paid the bills. Ida emptied the trash. Raymond did the laundry and vacuumed the rug. Everyone worked very hard.

Lesson F: Another view

Exercise 1 page 112

1. B   3. C   5. B
2. B   4. A   6. D

Exercise 2 page 113

1. A: Does Mom usually make dinner or do the laundry on Saturday?
   B: Mom usually does the laundry.
2. A: Does Annie usually make dinner or cut the grass on Saturday?
   B: Annie usually cuts the grass.
3. A: Does Dad usually cut the grass or mop the floor on Saturday?
   B: Dad usually mops the floor.
4. A: Does Grandma usually make dinner or mop the floor on Saturday?
   B: Grandma usually makes dinner.
5. A: Does Sam usually walk the dog or empty the trash on Saturday?
   B: Sam usually walks the dog.
6. A: Does Jessie usually empty the trash or mop the floor on Saturday?
   B: Jessie usually empties the trash.

Unit 10: Free time

Lesson A: Listening

Exercise 1 page 114

```
g o i n g o n a p i c n i c
i n g m g f w p l o m h k m
c a n o e i n g g i x o f i
r o n h c s g e c e p c e s
i c i a k h b k a f r a m l
c a n i i i y f m e q s g a
p h i k i n g i p a u w p t
i o f e i g n i x a i y e
c i l a g g k i n d y n o z
g s w i m m i n g f m b e l
```

Exercise 2 page 114

1. hiking   4. canoeing
2. swimming   5. camping
3. fishing   6. going on a picnic

Exercise 3 page 115

1. b   3. d   5. d
2. a   4. b   6. d

Exercise 4 page 115

1. yesterday
2. last weekend
3. last Saturday
4. last Sunday
5. last weekend
6. last week

Lesson B: What did you do yesterday?

Exercise 1 page 116

1. did   6. made
2. drove   7. read
3. ate   8. saw
4. went   9. slept
5. had   10. wrote

Exercise 2 page 116

1A. go   5A. drive
1B. went   5B. drove
2A. eat   6A. read
2B. ate   6B. read
3A. do   7A. sleep
3B. went   8A. see
4A. write   8B. saw